FIRST GRADE

Everything
for Early Learning

Thinking Kids®
Carson-Dellosa Publishing LLC
Greensboro, North Carolina

Thinking Kids®
Carson-Dellosa Publishing LLC
PO Box 35665
Greensboro, NC 27425 USA

Printed in the USA • All rights reserved.
01-082181151

ISBN 978-1-4838-3941-7

Table of Contents

Welcome to *Everything for Early Learning* for first grade! This book contains everything you and your child need for a creative approach to math and language arts practice. It gives you the tools to help fill knowledge gaps and build foundations that will prepare your child for higher-level math and language arts. Your child will learn to think about, apply, and reason with math and language arts concepts.

Everything for Early Learning is organized into eight sections based on the skills covered. Each activity supports the current state standards and offers a fun and active approach to essential first grade math and language arts skills. Creative and open-ended lessons offer concrete examples of math and language arts concepts to help promote understanding.

This book aims to increase critical thinking and problem solving skills with colorful and entertaining activities. Each activity supports early learning standards and encourages children to connect with essential math and language arts skills by showing their answers in different ways.

In *Everything for Early Learning,* your child will learn about:

- Numbers and operations
- Algebra
- Geometry
- Measurement
- Data analysis and probability
- Reading
- Reading comprehension
- English
- Spelling

Math

Cracker Count

Draw the correct number of crackers on each pan.

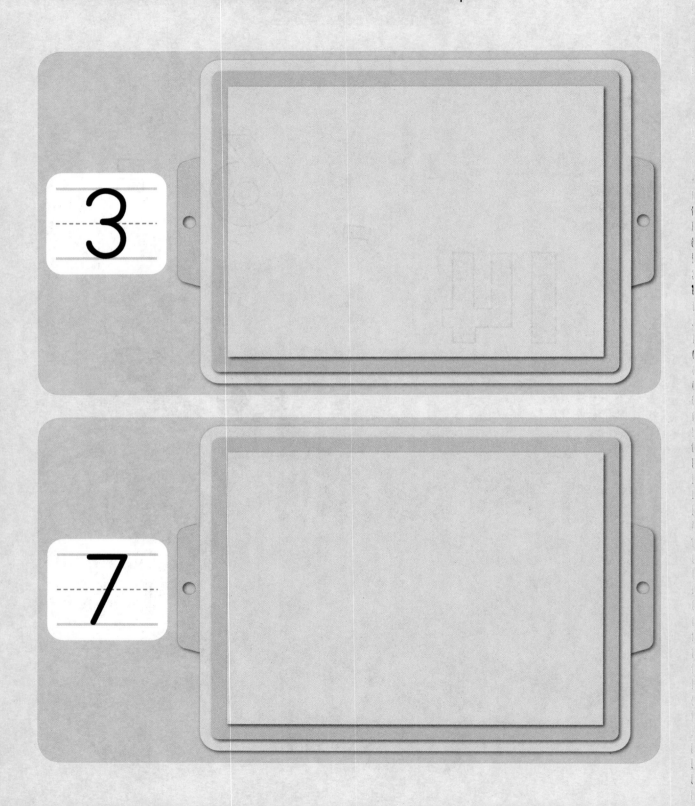

3

7

Look at the number. Catch that number of fish by circling the fish in the pond.

How Many Socks?

Count the socks in each row. Write the number of socks. Then, circle even or odd.

even

_____

odd

even

_____

odd

even

_____

odd

Balloon Bunches

Count the balloons. Write the number of tens and ones and the total. In the last box, draw balloons to show the tens and ones. Then, write the total.

_____ ten

_____ ones

_____ total

_____ ten

_____ ones

_____ total

2 tens

4 ones

_____ total

Balloon Bunches

Count the balloons. Write the number of tens and ones and the total. In the last box, draw balloons to show the tens and ones. Then, write the total.

_____ ten

_____ ones

_____ total

_____ ten

_____ ones

_____ total

__2__ tens

__2__ ones

_____ total

Pinball Numbers

Write numbers to complete the chart. The first one has been done for you.

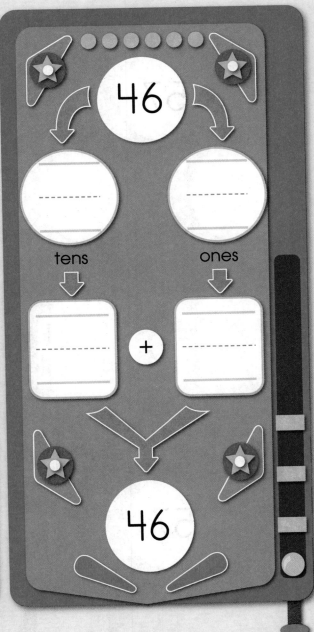

Pinball Numbers

Write numbers to complete the charts.

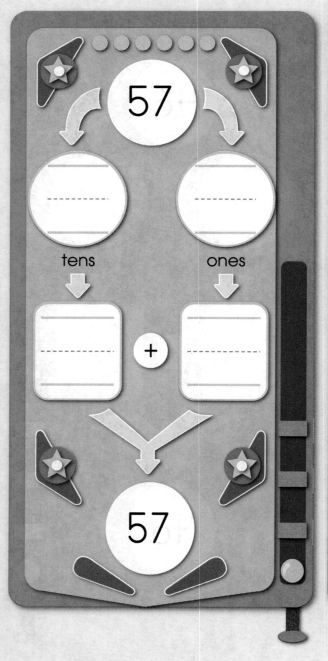

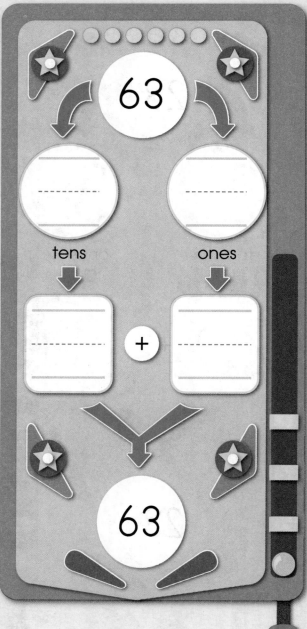

Peas and Carrots

Count the peas and carrots. Circle groups of 10. Write how many tens and ones. Write the total. Then, answer the question.

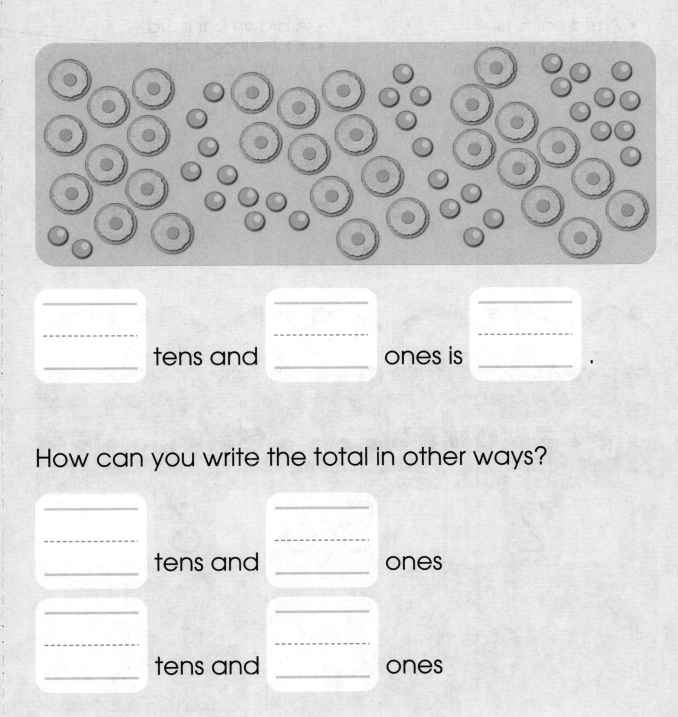

_____ tens and _____ ones is _____ .

How can you write the total in other ways?

_____ tens and _____ ones

_____ tens and _____ ones

Traffic Jam

Draw and color the correct cars. Write the missing number under each car.

- A red car is 1st.
- A blue car is 4th.
- A green car is 10th.

- A brown car is 3rd.
- A black car is 7th.
- A white car is 9th.

Speedy Snails

Write the number on each shell and the ordinal number word on each provided line to show the order the snails will finish the race.

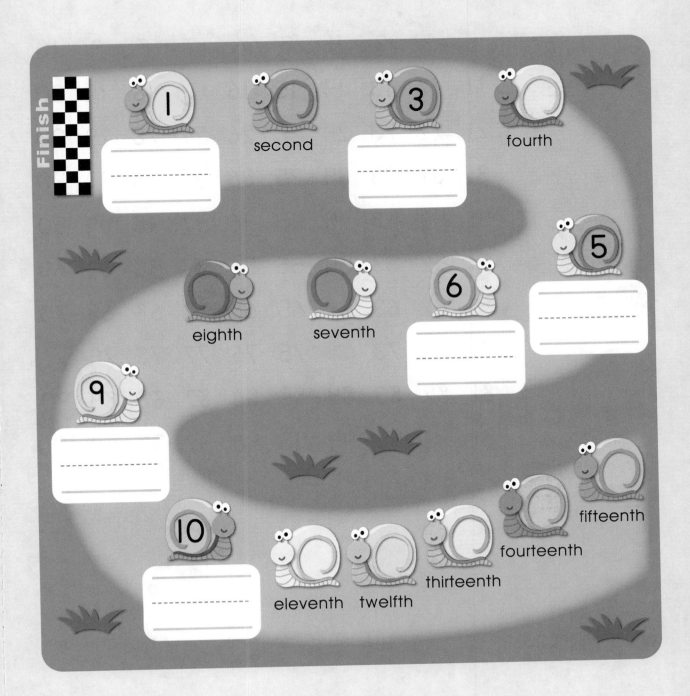

Everything for Early Learning 1

Puppy Playtime

Help the puppy count to 100. Write the number that is hidden under each object.

1	2	3	4	5	6	7	8	9	10
11	12	13	14	15	16		18	19	20
21	22	23	24		26	27	28	29	30
31	32	33	34	35	36	37	38	39	40
41	42	43	44	45	46	47	48	49	50
51	52	53	54	55	56	57	58	59	60
	62	63	64	65	66	67	68	69	70
71	72	73		75	76	77	78	79	
81	82	83	84	85	86	87	88	89	90
91	92	93	94	95	96	97	98	99	100

= _____

= _____

= _____

= _____

= _____

Square Subtraction

Use the hundred board to solve each problem. Circle the first number in the problem on the board. Then, draw a path on the board as you count back to subtract the second number. Draw a triangle around the answer. Write the answer to complete the number sentence.

$22 - 11 =$ _____ $67 - 14 =$ _____ $36 - 9 =$ _____

$88 - 12 =$ _____ $94 - 5 =$ _____ $51 - 12 =$ _____

1	2	3	4	5	6	7	8	9	10
11	12	13	14	15	16	17	18	19	20
21	22	23	24	25	26	27	28	29	30
31	32	33	34	35	36	37	38	39	40
41	42	43	44	45	46	47	48	49	50
51	52	53	54	55	56	57	58	59	60
61	62	63	64	65	66	67	68	69	70
71	72	73	74	75	76	77	78	79	80
81	82	83	84	85	86	87	88	89	90
91	92	93	94	95	96	97	98	99	100

Filling Flower Beds

Look at the number. Draw flowers in the 2 flower beds to show the number.

13

The More Door

Draw a door around the number that is greater on each house.

28 82

94 49

63 36

18 81

14 41

Everything for Early Learning 1

The More Door

Draw a door around the number that is greater on each house.

Read each number. Circle the correct number word. Show the number in 2 different ways using pictures, number sentences, or tally marks.

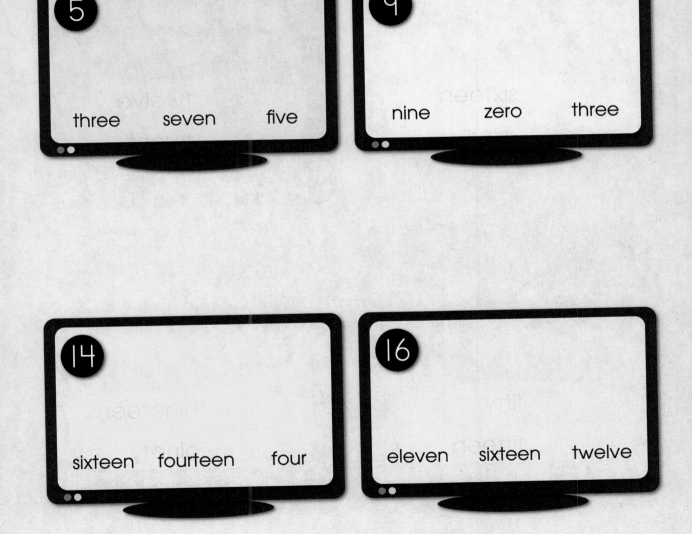

5
three   seven   five

9
nine   zero   three

14
sixteen   fourteen   four

16
eleven   sixteen   twelve

Bubble Counts

Count the bubbles in each bathtub. Write the number on the line. Circle the correct number word.

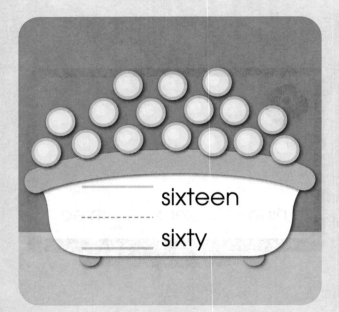

_____

sixteen

_____

sixty

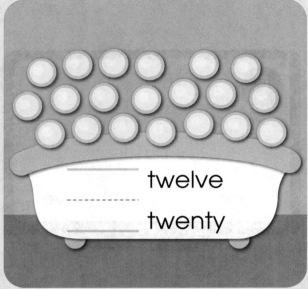

_____

twelve

_____

twenty

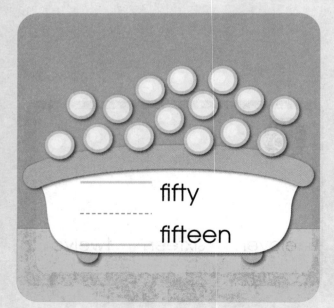

_____

fifty

_____

fifteen

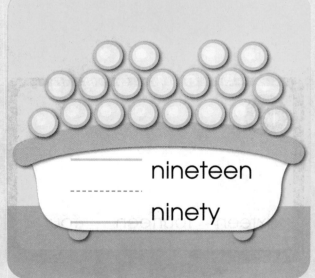

_____

nineteen

_____

ninety

Circle each pizza that shows equal parts.

Fraction Snacks

Draw lines to divide each snack into equal parts to show the bottom number of the fraction. Draw an X on one part to show the fraction.

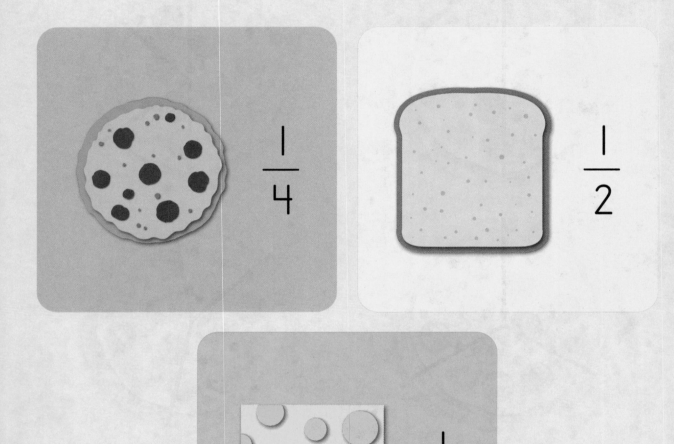

Draw lines to divide each snack into equal parts to show the bottom number of the fraction. Draw an X on one part to show the fraction.

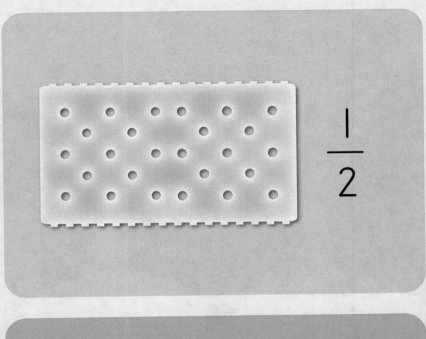

$\dfrac{1}{2}$

$\dfrac{1}{4}$

Apple Picking

Write the fractions of red and yellow apples in each tree. The first two have been started for you.

red	yellow	red	yellow	red	yellow
7	7	8	8		

Apple Picking

Write the fractions of red and yellow apples in each tree.

Nest Sets

Look at the numbers on the first and second nests. Draw eggs in the nests to show the numbers. Draw the correct number of eggs in the last nest to make the sum. Write the sum.

4 + 3 =

Nest Sets

Write a number below the first and second nests. Draw eggs in the nests to show the numbers. Draw the correct number of eggs in the last nest to make the sum. Write the sum.

Planting On

Count the vegetables in each row. Draw the correct number of vegetables to make the sum at the end of each row.

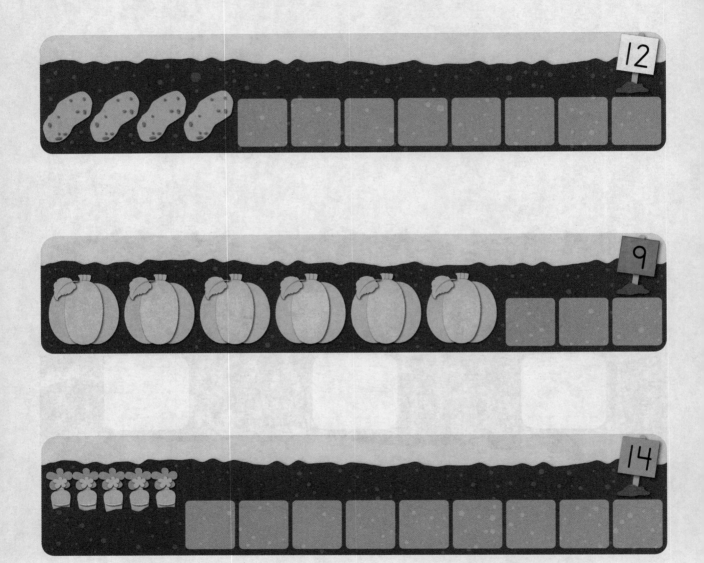

Count the vegetables in each row. Draw the correct number of vegetables to make the sum at the end of each row.

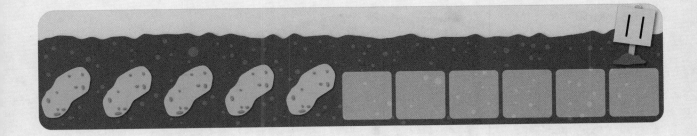

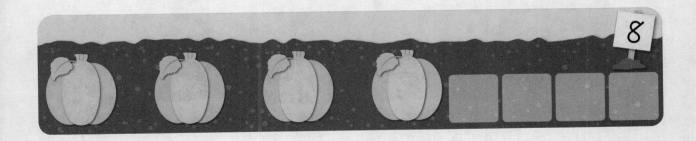

Bears' Lair

Draw 8 bears in the cave. Roll a die and subtract that many bears.
Write the number sentence. Repeat three more times.

_____ − _____ = _____   _____ − _____ = _____

_____ − _____ = _____   _____ − _____ = _____

Bears' Lair

Draw 10 bears in the cave. Roll a die and subtract that many bears.
Write the number sentence. Repeat three more times.

Frogs on a Log

Roll a die. Starting at 10, count back the rolled number as hops on the log. Write what you did as a subtraction fact. Repeat five more times.

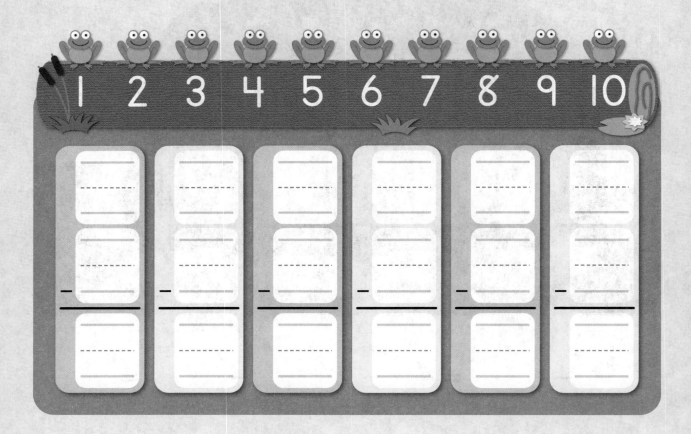

How Many More?

Count the gumballs in the pair of gumball machines. Write a number sentence to show how many more gumballs are in the first machine.

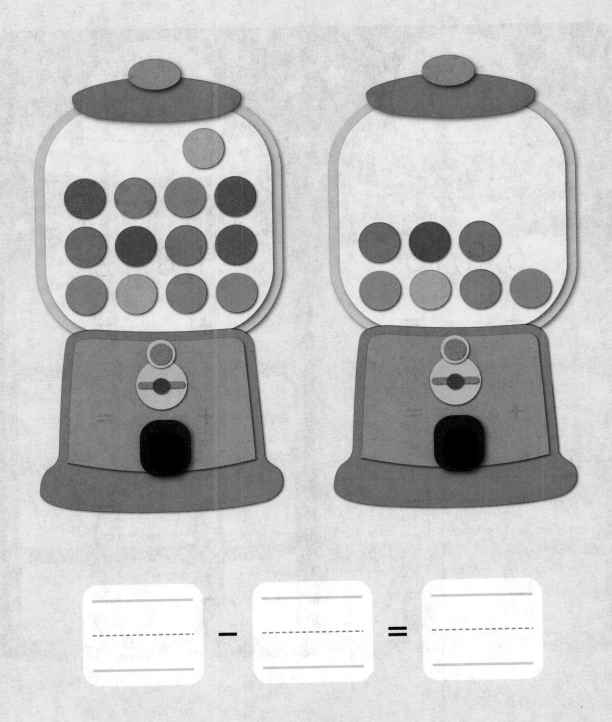

_____ - _____ = _____

Blastoff Facts

Write the four facts for each fact family.

6, 9, 15

_____ + _____ = _____

_____ + _____ = _____

_____ − _____ = _____

_____ − _____ = _____

4, 8, 12

_____ + _____ = _____

_____ + _____ = _____

_____ − _____ = _____

_____ − _____ = _____

Seeing Spots

Look at the domino in each box. Each domino represents a fact family. Write the related facts for each fact family.

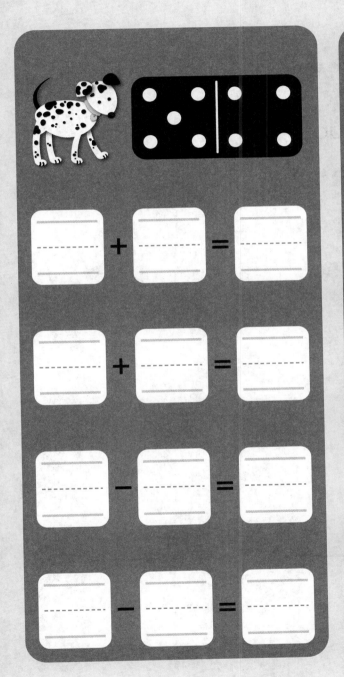

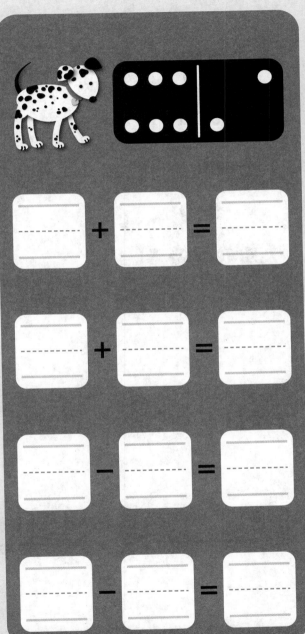

Basket of Cherries

Three children picked cherries. Add the three amounts of cherries that each child picked.

Mystery Signs

Write + or – to make each number sentence true.

$$9 \;\square\; 5 = 14$$

$$16 \;\square\; 9 = 7$$

Mystery Signs

Write + or – to make each number sentence true.

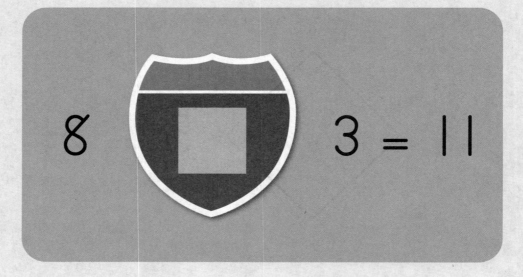

8 ⬜ 3 = 11

8 ⬜ 5 = 13

Count the acorns and peanuts. Divide each set of nuts into two equal groups so that the squirrels will have equal shares. Draw the nuts.

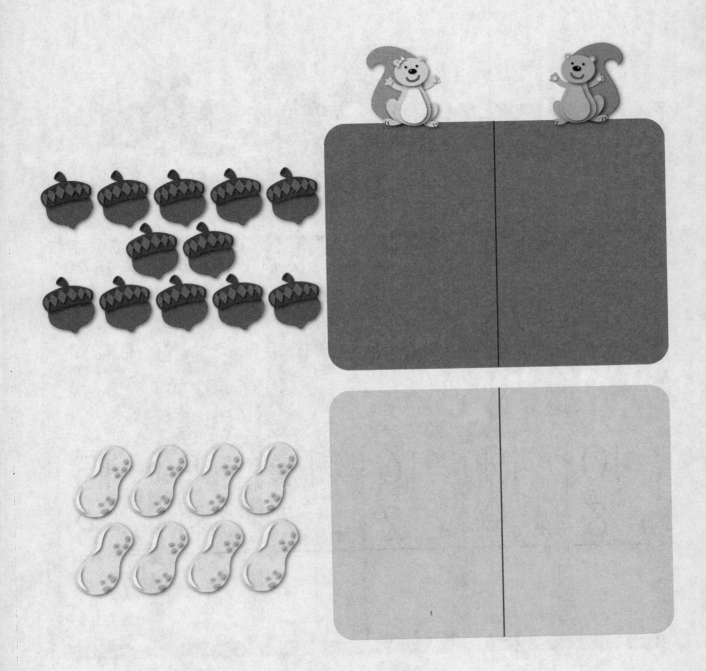

Adventure Island

Count on to solve each problem. The common sum is the spot where the pirate buried his treasure. Mark the spot on the number line with an X.

0 1 2 3 4 5 6 7 8 9 10 11 12 13 14 15 16 17 18 19 20

| 10 | 14 | 16 | 11 | 9 | 15 |
+ 8	+ 4	+ 2	+ 7	+ 9	+ 3

Adventure Island

Count on to solve each problem. The common sum is the spot where the pirate buried his treasure. Mark the spot on the number line with an X.

$$10 + 6 = \underline{\hspace{2cm}}$$

$$12 + 4 = \underline{\hspace{2cm}}$$

$$14 + 2 = \underline{\hspace{2cm}}$$

$$11 + 5 = \underline{\hspace{2cm}}$$

$$8 + 8 = \underline{\hspace{2cm}}$$

$$13 + 3 = \underline{\hspace{2cm}}$$

Flip It!

Solve each addition problem. Use the addition facts to help you solve each subtraction problem.

18 − 9 = [____] → THINK → 9 + [____] = 18

14 − 6 = [____] → THINK → 6 + [____] = 14

17 − 8 = [____] → THINK → 8 + [____] = 17

15 − 7 = [____] → THINK → 7 + [____] = 15

Flip It!

Solve each addition problem. Use the addition facts to help you solve each subtraction problem.

18 − 8 = _____ → **THINK** → 8 + _____ = 18

14 − 5 = _____ → **THINK** → 5 + _____ = 14

17 − 6 = _____ → **THINK** → 6 + _____ = 17

15 − 4 = _____ → **THINK** → 4 + _____ = 15

More or Less

Start with the middle number. Write the numbers that are 1 more and 2 more. Then, write the numbers that are 1 less and 2 less.

Two Color Sums

Use two different colors of crayons to color each row. Then, write two addition facts that show the color amounts.

_____ + _____ = 10   _____ + _____ = 10

_____ + _____ = 8   _____ + _____ = 8

_____ + _____ = 12   _____ + _____ = 12

Dip Into Dominoes

Count the dots on each side of each domino. Then, write the related facts for each domino.

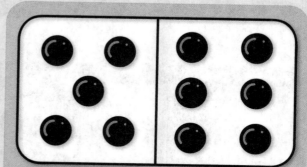

____ + ____ = ____

____ + ____ = ____

____ − ____ = ____

____ − ____ = ____

____ + ____ = ____

____ + ____ = ____

____ − ____ = ____

____ − ____ = ____

Subtraction Squares

Subtract each row and then each column. Write the answers on the lines.

11	6	___
3	2	___
___	___	___

14	7	___
5	4	___
___	___	___

16	8	___
9	4	___
___	___	___

Subtraction Squares

Subtract each row and then each column. Write the answers on the lines.

10	4	____
3	2	____
____	____	____

13	8	____
5	4	____
____	____	____

15	7	____
9	4	____
____	____	____

Jelly Bean Math

Draw or cross out jelly beans in each frame to make the number.

Make 9

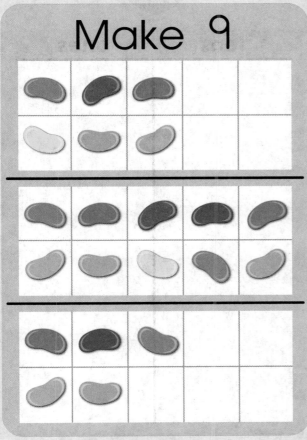

Make 6

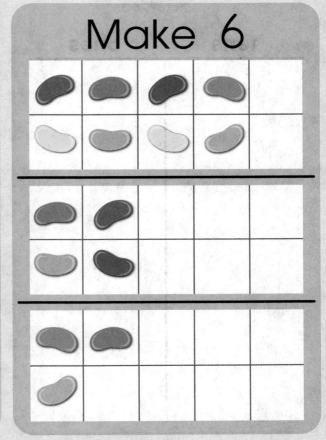

A Number of Ways

Draw a picture of how you would model each number using base ten blocks. Write the number of tens and ones in the blanks.

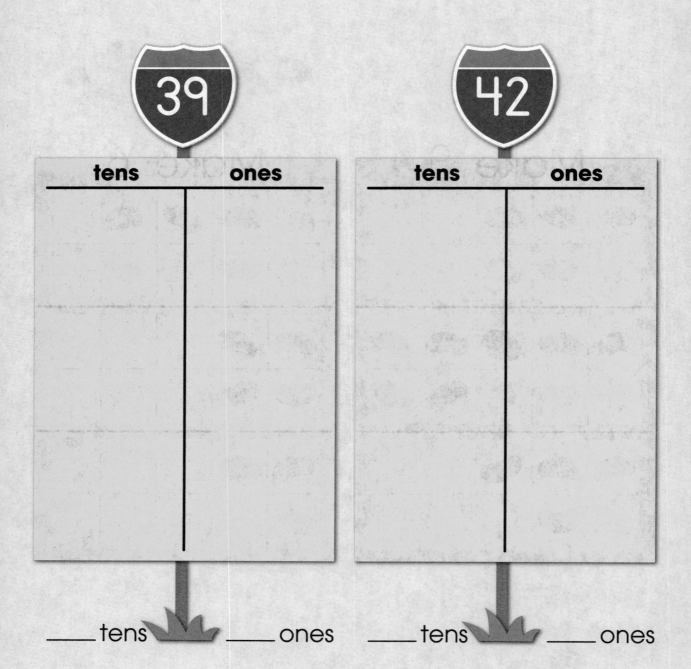

39

tens	ones

____ tens ____ ones

42

tens	ones

____ tens ____ ones

Draw a picture of how you would model each number using base ten blocks. Write the number of tens and ones in the blanks.

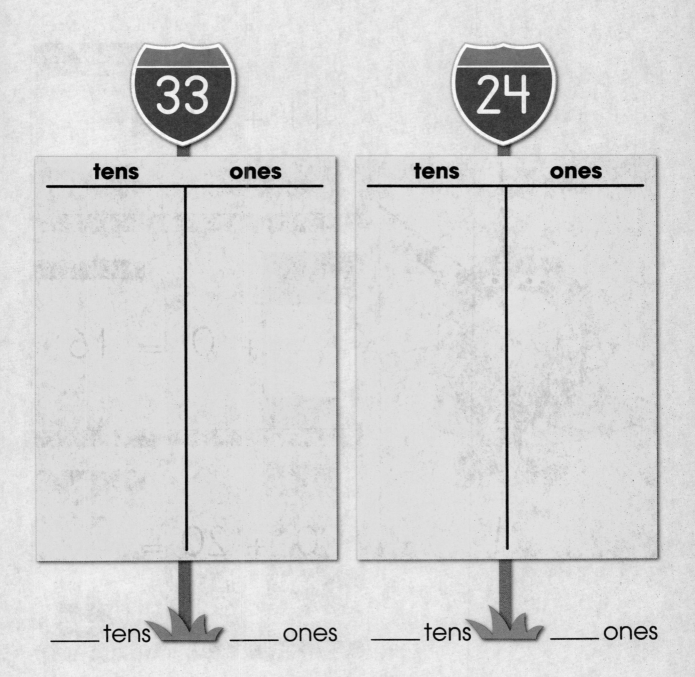

33	
tens	**ones**

24	
tens	**ones**

___ tens   ___ ones   ___ tens   ___ ones

Zero the Hero

Write each missing number to complete the addition facts with zero.

$11 + 0 = $ _____

_____ $+ 0 = 16$

$0 + 20 = $ _____

Bubble, Bubble

Color each pair of bubbles that have the same sum. Use a different color for each pair.

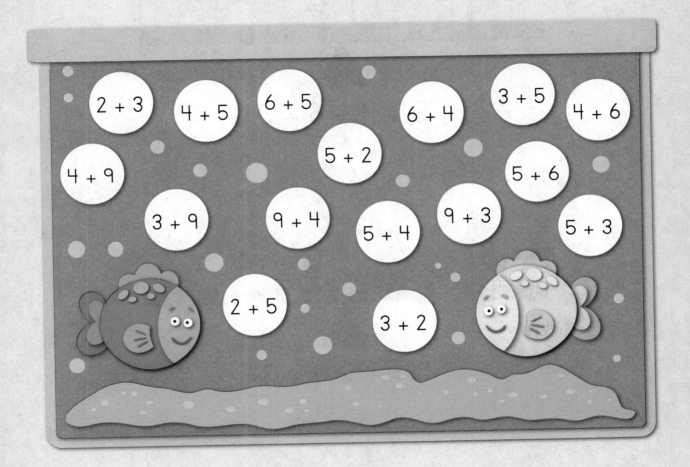

Seesaw Sums

Draw stars on each side of the seesaw to test each equation. Circle the equations that are true. Cross out the equations that are not true.

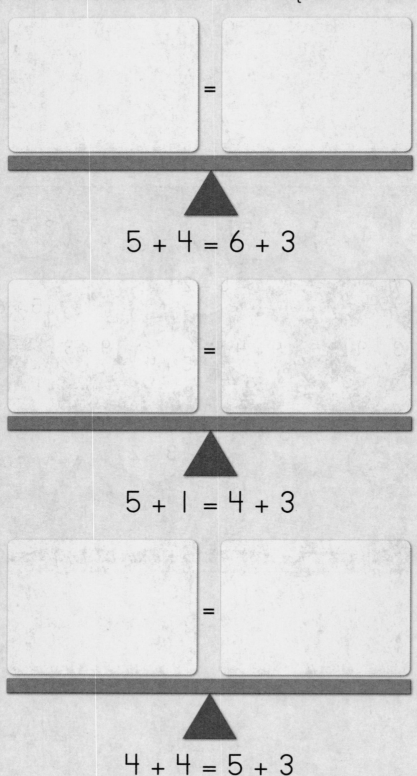

$$5 + 4 = 6 + 3$$

$$5 + 1 = 4 + 3$$

$$4 + 4 = 5 + 3$$

Tipping the Scales

Look at the numbers below each scale. Write >, <, or = to compare each set of numbers.

> greater than   **<** less than   **=** equal to

6 + 2 ☐ 10

9 + 9 ☐ 18

13 ☐ 9 + 2

Choose two characteristics. Write them on the lines. Sort the fish by writing their numbers in the bowls.

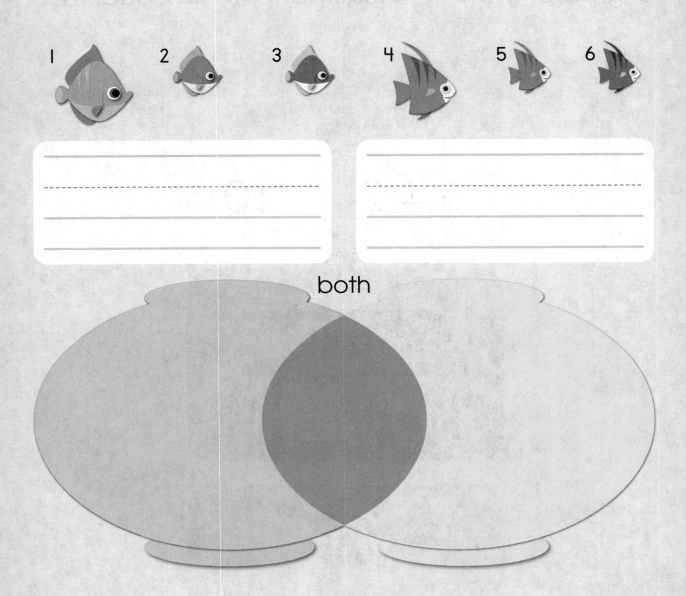

both

Draw an X on the object in each row that does not belong.

Quilt Patterns

Put pennies on the squares in each row to make a pattern that matches.

Patterns, Patterns

Circle the object that comes next in each pattern.

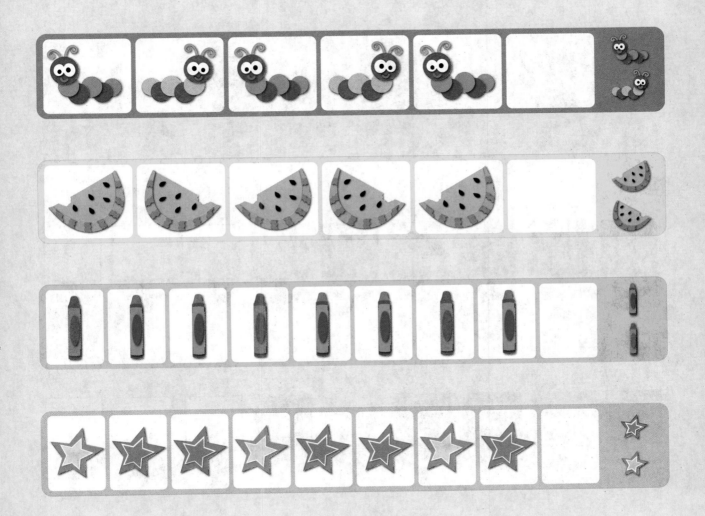

A Garden of Patterns

Color the squares to complete each pattern.

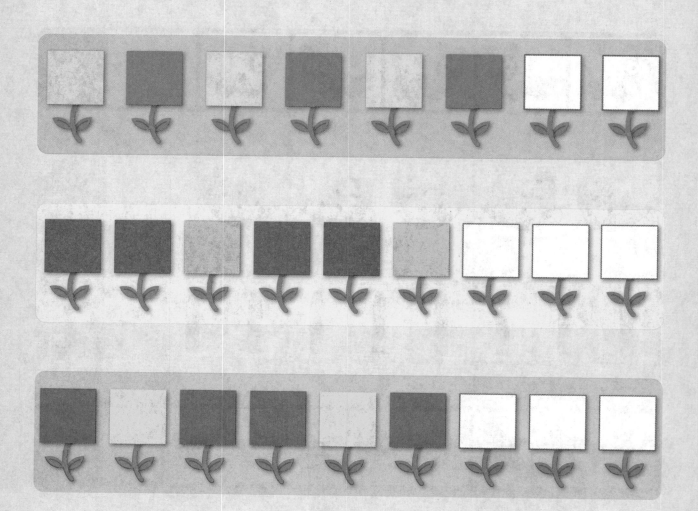

Copy Cat

Name each pattern with the letters A and B. Then, draw and color cats to copy the pattern.

Everything for Early Learning 1

Bead Patterns

Say each bead pattern. Then, answer the questions.

What color is the missing bead?

If this pattern continues, what color will the 15th bead be?

What color are the missing beads?

If this pattern continues, what color will the 12th bead be?

Keisha's Bracelets

Keisha made two bracelets. Color the blank beads to show each pattern.

She made an AB pattern with 4 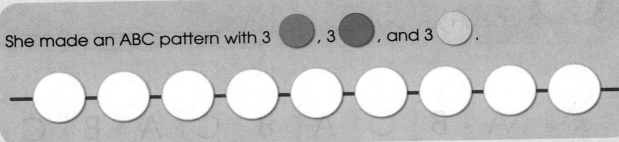 and 4 ⬤.

She made an ABC pattern with 3 ⬤, 3 ⬤, and 3 ⚪.

Each child named the shape pattern in a different way. Explain each child's rule.

Sara

A	A	B	A	A	B	A	A	B

Explain Sara's rule: _____

Gabe

A	B	C	A	B	C	A	B	C

Explain Gabe's rule: _____

Growing Patterns

Finish each pattern.

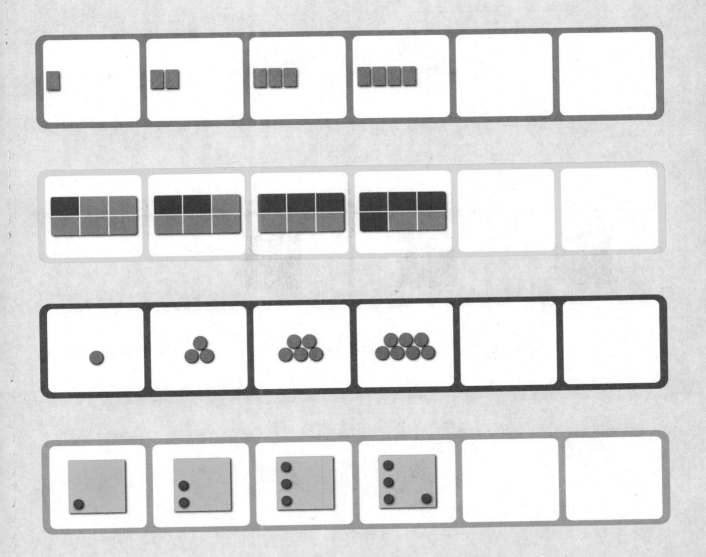

Draw what comes next in each pattern.

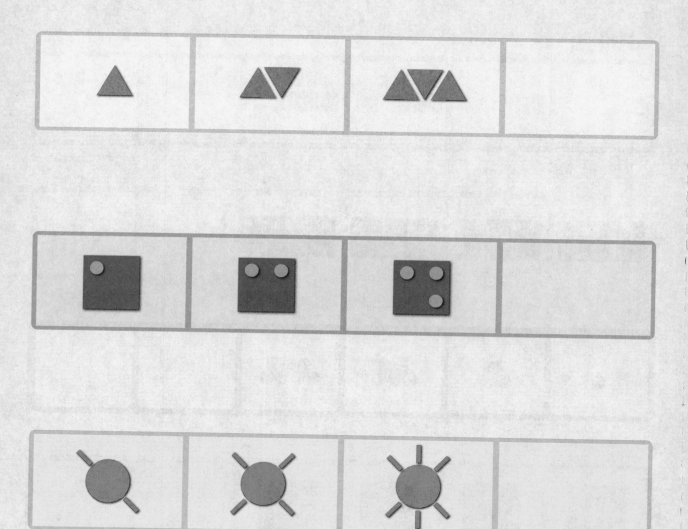

Puppy Patterns

Name each pattern using letters. Then, draw and color dogs to copy the pattern.

Everything for Early Learning 1

Draw the shape that comes next in each pattern. Tell whether the shape was slid, turned, or flipped.

Bead a Pattern

Color the blank beads to continue each pattern.

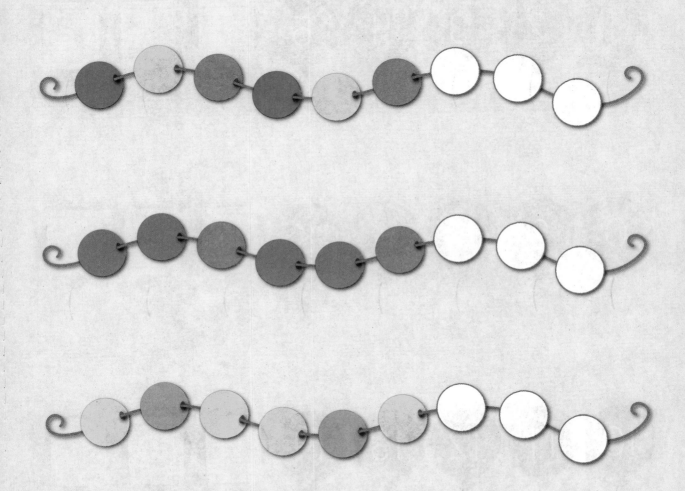

Finish each pattern.

Petal Patterns

Study each number pattern. Start at the dot. Write the rule.

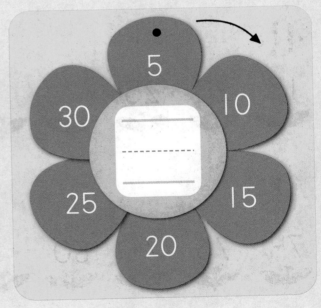

Buzzing Around

Write the missing numbers in each row of flowers.

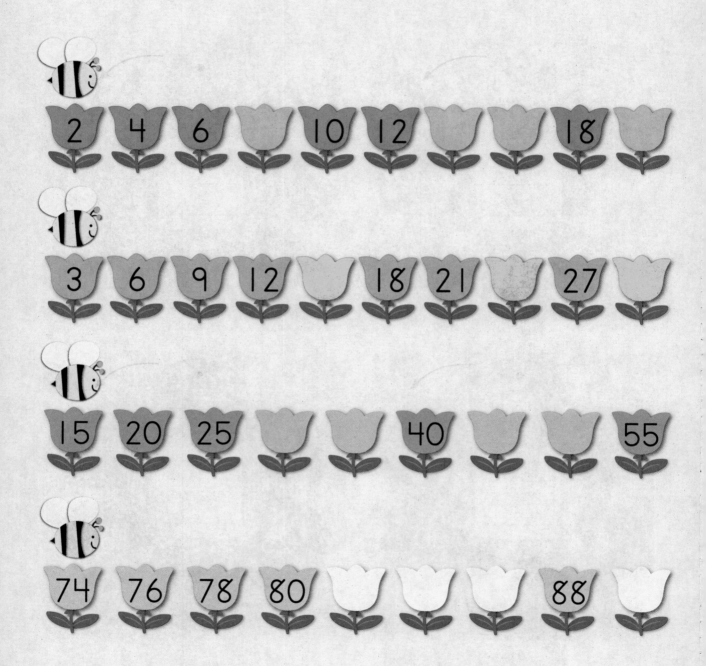

2   4   6   ___   10   12   ___   ___   18   ___

3   6   9   12   ___   18   21   ___   27   ___

15   20   25   ___   ___   40   ___   ___   55

74   76   78   80   ___   ___   ___   88   ___

Name that Figure!

Circle the word that describes each object.

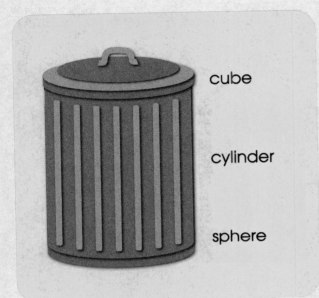

cube

cylinder

sphere

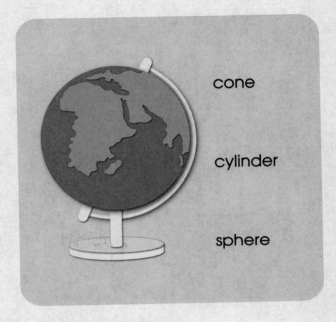

cone

cylinder

sphere

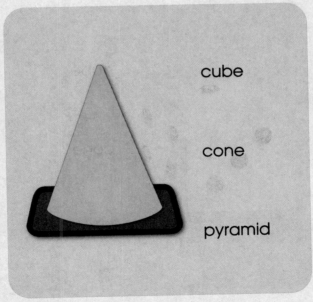

cube

cone

pyramid

Circle the word that describes each object.

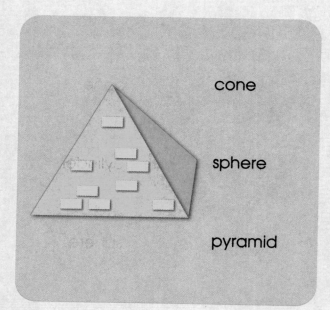

cone

sphere

pyramid

sphere

cone

rectangular prism

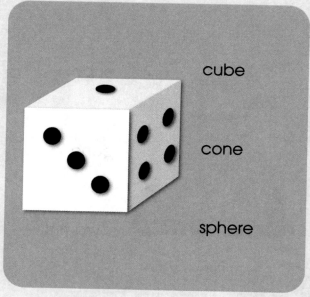

cube

cone

sphere

Shapes Rule!

Draw some shapes by each rule. Then, write your own sorting rules and sort the shapes.

Straight Sides	Four Corners	
		_____
		_____
Curvy Sides	More or Less Than Four Corners	
		_____

The Great Shape Sort

Follow the directions.

1. Color each circle.

2. Outline each shape that has 4 sides.

3. Circle each small shape.

4. Draw an X on each square.

5. Draw a dot in each shape with 3 sides.

Angles, Faces, and Sides

Read each description. Circle the correct figure. You may circle more than one figure in each row.

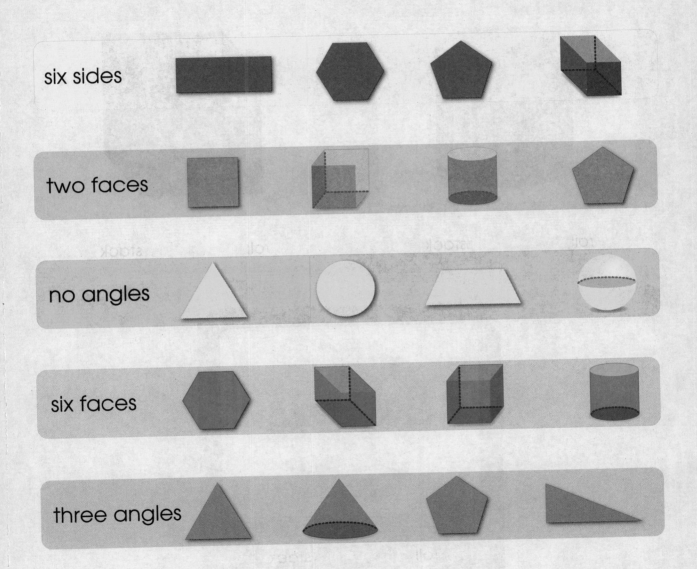

six sides

two faces

no angles

six faces

three angles

Look at each figure. Decide if it will roll, stack, or do both. Circle the answer(s).

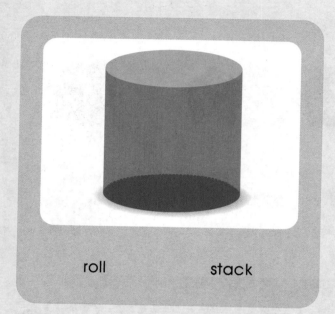

roll   stack

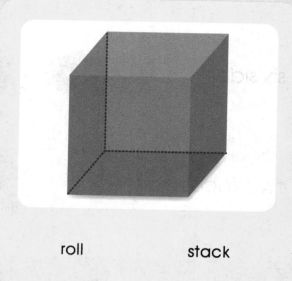

roll   stack

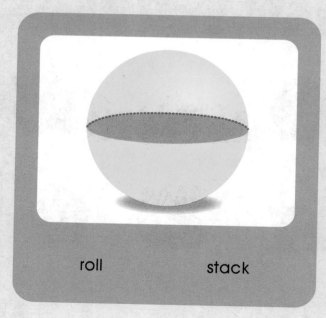

roll   stack

Shape Creations

Circle the shapes needed to make each picture.

Castle Shapes

Describe where each shape is. Use color words, shape names, and position words.

Beth's Beagle

Follow the directions to help Beth find her dog. Write the missing words in the directions as you go. Draw an X where she finds the dog.

Walk past 2 trees. Turn right and walk to the house.

Turn left and walk to the _____.

Turn right and walk to the _____.

Turn right and walk past the pond.

Turn right and walk to the _____.

Turn left and walk to the end of the garden.

Turn left and walk straight to find the dog.

The dog is in the _____.

START

Where's the Bear?

Use numbers, letters, and shape names to describe where the bear is.

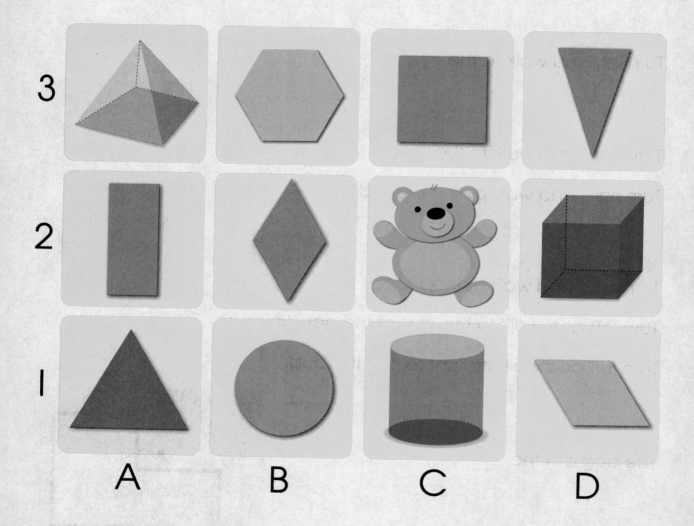

Draw how each shape would look after a flip, a slide, and a turn.

Shape	Flip	Slide	Turn

Circle the shapes and letters that have symmetry.

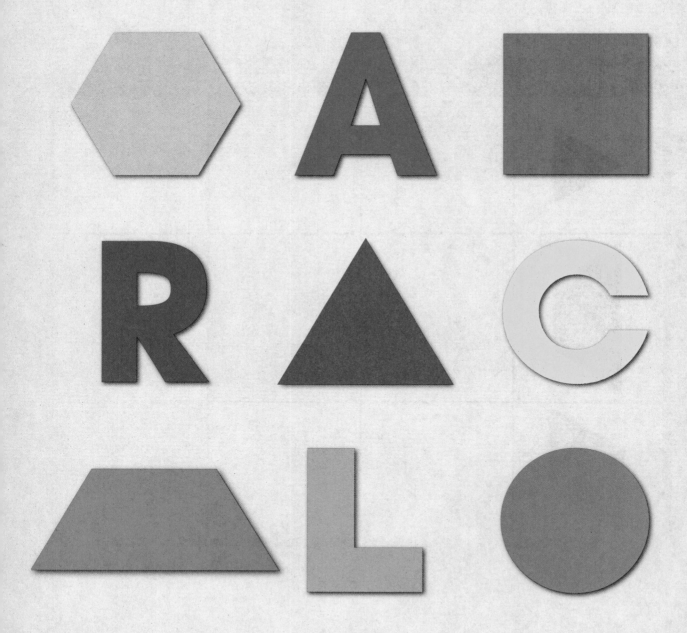

Circle each letter of the alphabet that has symmetry. Draw Xs on the letters that do not have symmetry.

Draw how each letter would look after a slide, a flip, and a turn.

| H | slide | flip | turn |

| P | slide | flip | turn |

| S | slide | flip | turn |

| T | slide | flip | turn |

Find that Face!

Circle the shape of the bottom face of each figure.

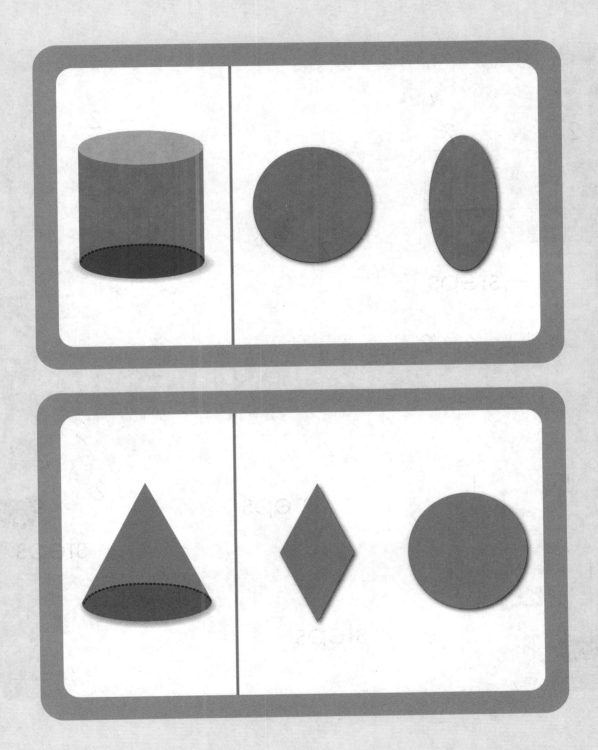

Picnic Perimeters

Write how many total steps it will take for each ant to walk around his picnic blanket.

steps

steps

steps

steps

Will's Worms

Will found some worms in his backyard. Use two fingers at a time to measure each worm.

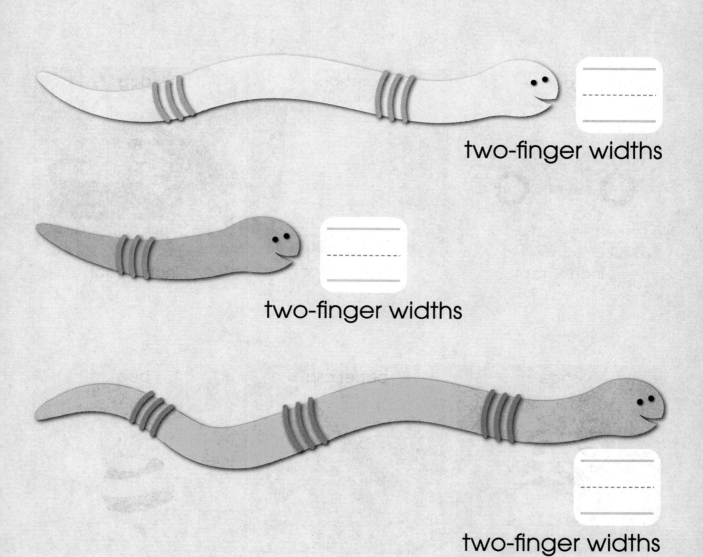

two-finger widths

two-finger widths

two-finger widths

two-finger widths

Circle the unit of measurement that best measures each object.

car	notebook	dog

inch foot	inch foot	inch foot

shoe	paper clip	bee

centimeter meter	centimeter meter	centimeter meter

Ribbon Measurement

Use the width of your thumb to measure the length of each ribbon.

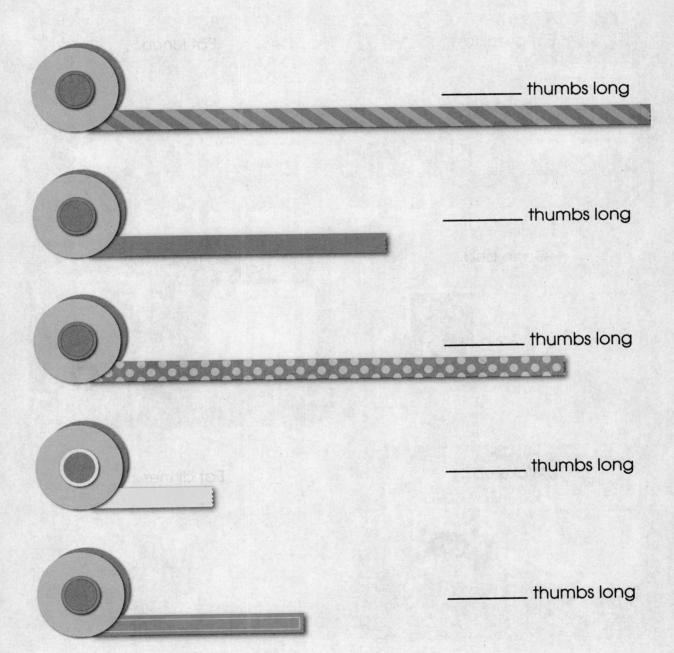

_____ thumbs long

_____ thumbs long

_____ thumbs long

_____ thumbs long

_____ thumbs long

Number the events from 1 to 6 in the order in which they occur.

Eat breakfast.

Eat lunch.

Go to bed.

Go to school.

Wake up.

Eat dinner.

The Hands of Time

Draw the hands or write the numbers to show the time for each clock.

The Hands of Time

Draw the hands or write the numbers to show the time for each clock.

Time and Time Again

Read the times. Draw the hands and write the numbers for each time given.

five o'clock

one thirty

seven o'clock

Read the times. Draw the hands and write the numbers for each time given.

three thirty

eight thirty

two o'clock

Elapsed Laps

Read each word problem. Draw the hands on the first clock to show the start time for the swimmer's laps. Draw the hands on the last clock to show the end time for the laps.

Start  **End**

Katie arrived at swim practice at 3:30. She swam her warm-up laps in 30 minutes. What time did she finish?

Start  **End**

Brady arrived at swim practice at 4:00. He finished his warm-up laps in 30 minutes. What time did he finish?

Start  **End**

Ethan arrived at swim practice at 3:00. He finished his warm-up laps in 30 minutes. What time did he finish?

Elapsed Laps

Read each word problem. Draw the hands on the first clock to show the start time for the swimmer's laps. Draw the hands on the last clock to show the end time for the laps.

Start

Jen arrived at swim practice at 4:30. She swam her warm-up laps in 30 minutes. What time did she finish?

End

Start

Scott arrived at swim practice at 5:00. He finished his warm-up laps in 30 minutes. What time did he finish?

End

Start

Adam arrived at swim practice at 2:30. He finished his warm-up laps in 30 minutes. What time did he finish?

End

Ants to Elephants

Number the animals from 1 to 6 to order them from lightest to heaviest.

chicken

frog

elephant

ant

dog

cow

A Balancing Act

Write the names of two objects or draw two objects on each scale to make the picture true.

Draw shapes in each box that have something in common with the shape pictured.

Pencil Poll Pictograph

Jon took a poll of four friends to see how many pencils each had in his or her pencil box. Use Jon's tally chart to draw the pencils in the graph.

James	ЖI	Lisa	IIII
Tony	II	Anya	IIII

James

Tony

Lisa

Anya

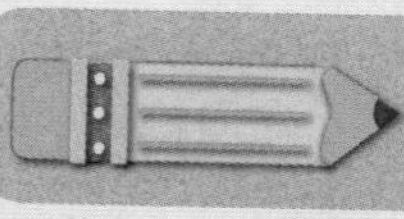

= 1 pencil

Backyard Bugs

Lin counted the bugs she collected in her backyard. Draw Xs in the spaces above each bug to make a bar graph of her data.

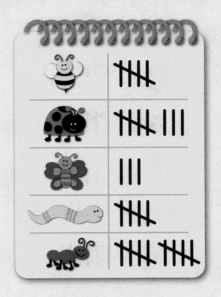

Backyard Bugs

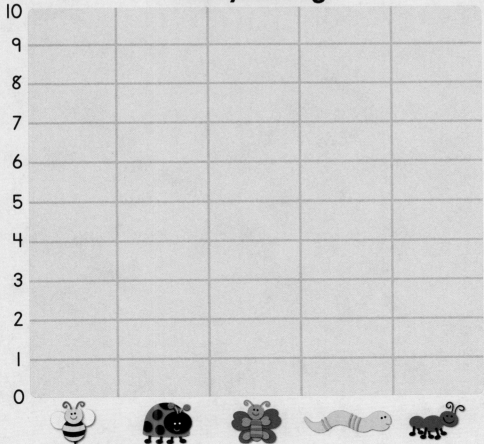

Picnic Time

Brian counted the items at the picnic. Draw Xs in the spaces above each item to make a bar graph of his data.

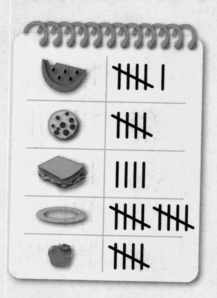

Picnic Items

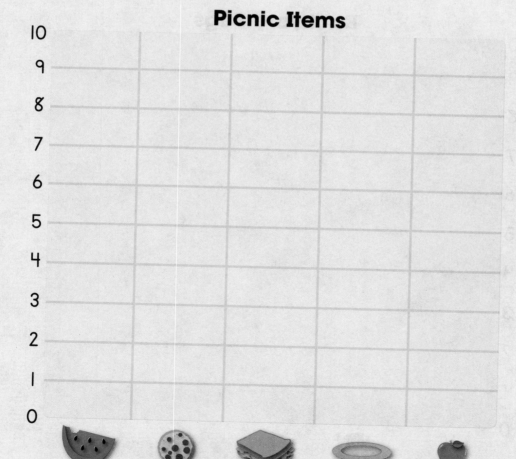

Preferred Pets

Look at the results of a class survey about favorite pets. Draw smiley faces to show the data in a pictograph. Look at the key to see how many votes each smiley face stands for.

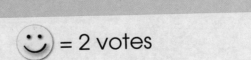
= 2 votes

Animal Graphs

Study the graph. Then, answer the questions.

What do the pictures show?
   a. trees
   b. animals
   c. people

Write a title above the graph.

Write two facts from the graph.

Mr. Kent's class kept track of the daily weather on the calendar last month. Use the calendar to answer the questions.

April

Sunday	Monday	Tuesday	Wednesday	Thursday	Friday	Saturday
					1	2
3	4	5	6	7	8	9
10	11	12	13	14	15	16
17	18	19	20	21	22	23
24	25	26	27	28	29	30

How many days were rainy?

How many days were cloudy but not rainy?

How many days were sunny?

How many days are in the month?

Circle likely or unlikely to answer each question.

If you were playing a game with this spinner, is it **likely** or **unlikely** that you would spin red?

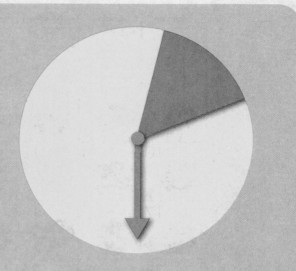

likely   unlikely

If you picked a marble out of this bag without looking, is it **likely** or **unlikely** that you would pick a red one?

likely   unlikely

Wishing Well

Decide how likely it is that a tossed coin will land on each well. Below each well, write more likely, likely, or less likely.

Language Arts

Name, Address, Phone

This book belongs to

I live at

The city I live in is

The state I live in is

My phone number is

Practice writing the letters.

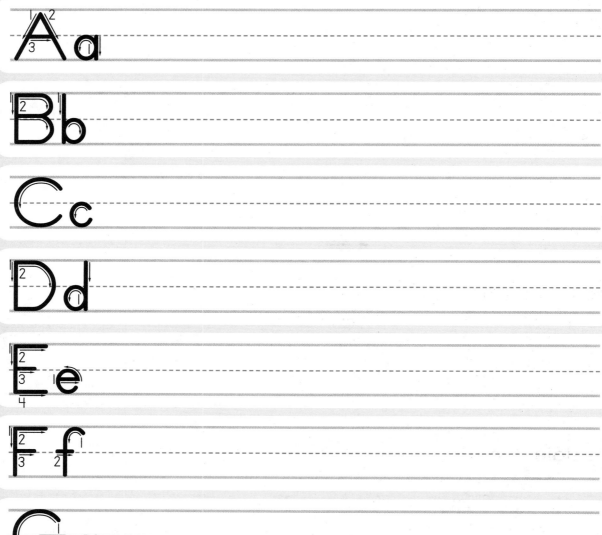

Practice writing the letters.

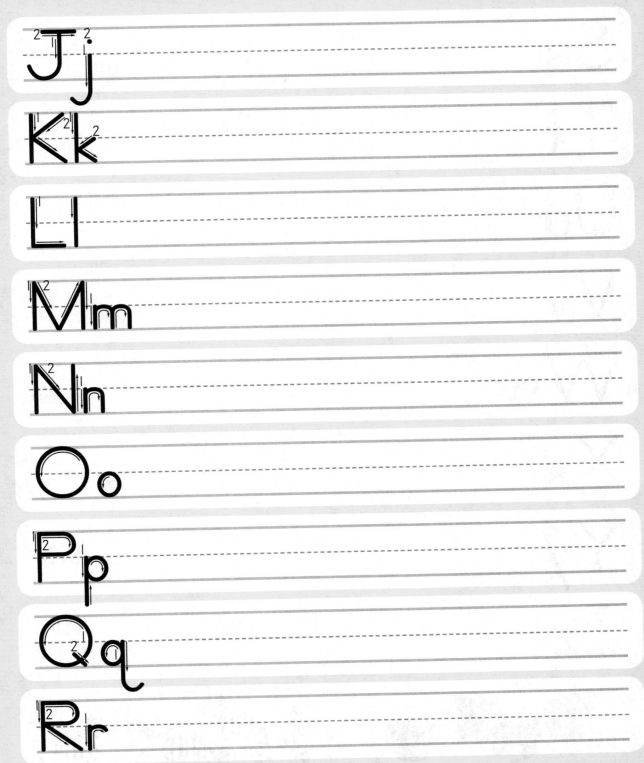

Practice writing the letters.

Ss

Tt

Uu

Vv

Ww

Xx

Yy

Zz

In each set, match the lowercase letter to the uppercase letter.

a	C
f	H
c	J
h	E
e	A
j	F
g	D
b	B
i	M
d	G
k	I
l	L
m	K

Letter Recognition

In each set, match the lowercase letter to the uppercase letter.

n	U
s	P
p	R
u	Q
r	N
q	S
t	V
y	O
v	T
o	W
x	Z
w	Y
z	X

Beginning consonants are the sounds that come at the beginning of words. Consonants are the letters b, c, d, f, g, h, j, k, l, m, n, p, q, r, s, t, v, w, x, y, and z.

Say the name of each letter. Say the sound each letter makes. Circle the letters that make the beginning sound for each picture. Then, color the pictures.

Bb

Cc

Dd

Ff

Bb Dd

Ff Cc

Cc Dd

Ff Bb

Bb Dd

Ff Cc

Cc Dd

Ff Bb

Beginning Consonants: Gg, Hh, Jj, Kk

Say the name of each letter. Say the sound each letter makes. Trace the letter pair that makes the beginning sound in each picture. Then, color the pictures.

Gg **Hh** **Jj** **Kk**

Kk   Hh   Gg   Kk

Gg   Hh   Jj   Gg

Say the name of each letter. Say the sound each letter makes. Trace the letter pair that makes the beginning sound in each picture. Then, color the pictures.

Say the name of each letter. Say the sound each letter makes. Trace the letter pair in the boxes. Then, color the picture that begins with that sound.

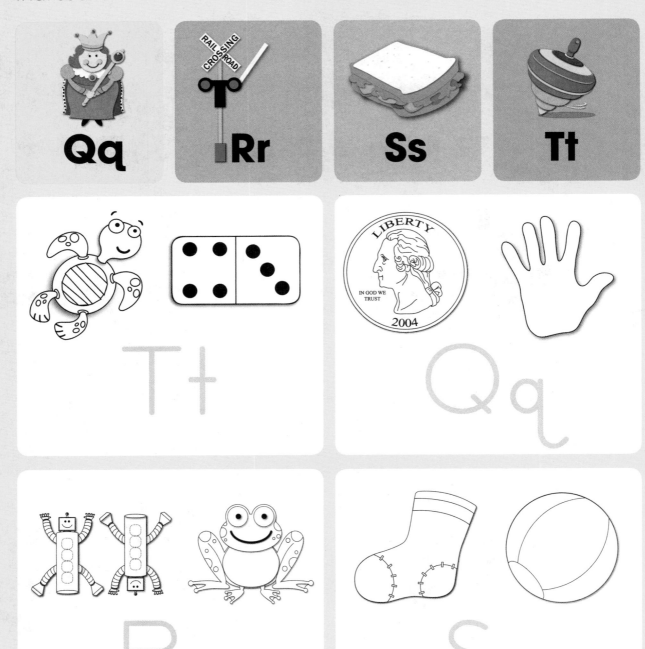

Say the name of each letter. Say the sound each letter makes. Trace the letters. Then, draw a line from each letter pair to the picture that begins with that sound.

 **Vv**  **Ww**  **Xx**  **Yy**  **Zz**

Beginning Consonants

Write the letter that makes the beginning sound for each picture.

_____ ift

_____ alloon

_____ oy

_____ irl

_____ ice

_____ at

_____ ird

_____ ouse

_____ og

Say the name of each picture. Draw a line from each letter to the pictures that end with that sound. Then, color the pictures.

Ending Consonants: k, l, p

Trace the letter in each row. Say the name of each picture. Then, color the pictures in each row that end with that sound.

Ending Consonants: r, s, t, x

Say the name of each picture. Then, circle the ending sound for each picture.

r s t x

r s t x

r s t x

r s t x

r s t x

r s t x

r s t x

r s t x

Short Vowel Sounds

Vowels are the letters **a**, **e**, **i**, **o**, and **u**. Short **a** is the sound you hear in **ant**. Short **e** is the sound you hear in **elephant**. Short **i** is the sound you hear in **igloo**. Short **o** is the sound you hear in **octopus**. Short **u** is the sound you hear in **umbrella**.

Write **a**, **e**, **i**, **o**, or **u** in each blank to finish the word. Draw a line from the word to the picture. Then, color the pictures.

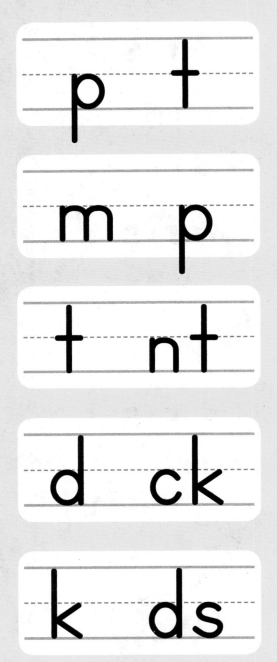

Long Vowel Sounds

Vowels are the letters **a, e, i, o,** and **u**. Long vowel sounds say their own names. Long **a** is the sound you hear in **hay**. Long **e** is the sound you hear in **me**. Long **i** is the sound you hear in **pie**. Long **o** is the sound you hear in **no**. Long **u** is the sound you hear in **cute**.

Write **a, e, i, o,** or **u** in each blank to finish the word. Draw a line from the word to the picture. Then, color the pictures.

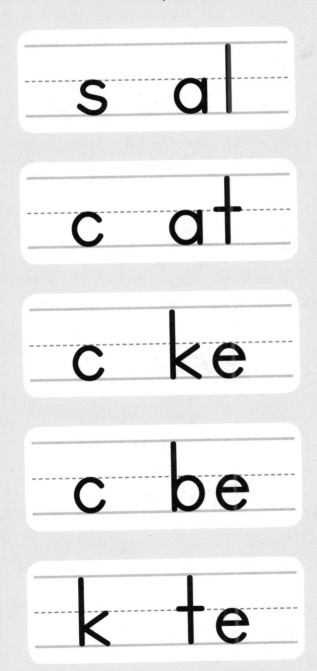

s a l

c a t

c ke

c be

k te

Short **a** sounds like the **a** in **hat**. Long **a** sounds like the **a** in **cape**.

Say the name of each picture. If it has the short **a** sound, color it **red**. If it has the long **a** sound, color it **yellow**.

Short and Long Ee

Short **e** sounds like the **e** in **hen**. Long **e** sounds like the **e** in **bee**.

Say the name of each picture. Circle the pictures that have the short **e** sound. Draw a triangle around the pictures that have a long **e** sound. Then, color the pictures.

Short and Long Ii

Short **i** sounds like the **i** in **pig**. Long **i** sounds like the **i** in **kite**.

Say the name of each picture. If it has the short **i** sound, color it **yellow**. If it has the long **i** sound, color it **red**.

Short **o** sounds like the **o** in **dog**. Long **o** sounds like the **o** in **rope**. Draw a line from the picture to the word that names it. Draw a circle around the word if it has a short **o** sound.

dog

globe

block

octopus

clock

Short and Long Uu

Short **u** sounds like the **u** in **bug**. Long **u** sounds like the **u** in **blue**.

Say the name of each picture. If it has the short **u** sound, color it **green**. If it has the long **u** sound, color it **purple**.

Write the correct vowel on the line to complete each word.

a   e   i   o   u

 c __ t

 d __ g

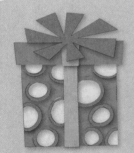 g __ f t

 b __ b

 s __ n

 c __ w

 s n __ w

 g __ __ t

Consonant Blends

Consonant blends are two or more consonant sounds together in a word. The blend is made by combining the consonant sounds.

Example: floor

The name of each picture begins with a **blend**. Circle the beginning blend for each picture. Then, color the pictures.

bl   fl   cl

cl   fl   gl

fl   bl   pl

fl   cl   gl

pl   gl   cl

gl   fl   cl

Consonant Blends

Draw a line from the picture to the blend that begins its name. Then, color the pictures.

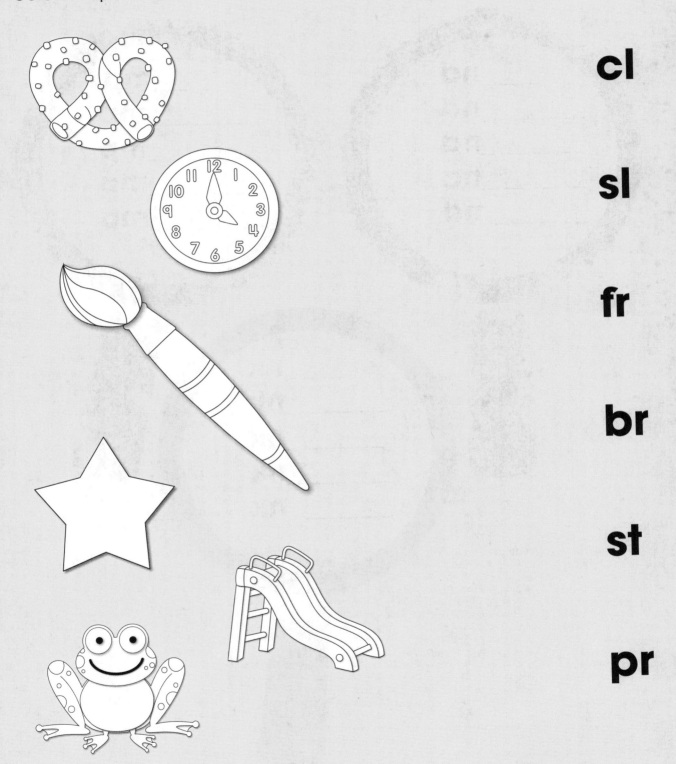

cl

sl

fr

br

st

pr

Ending Consonant Blends

Add letters to the word endings to create new words.

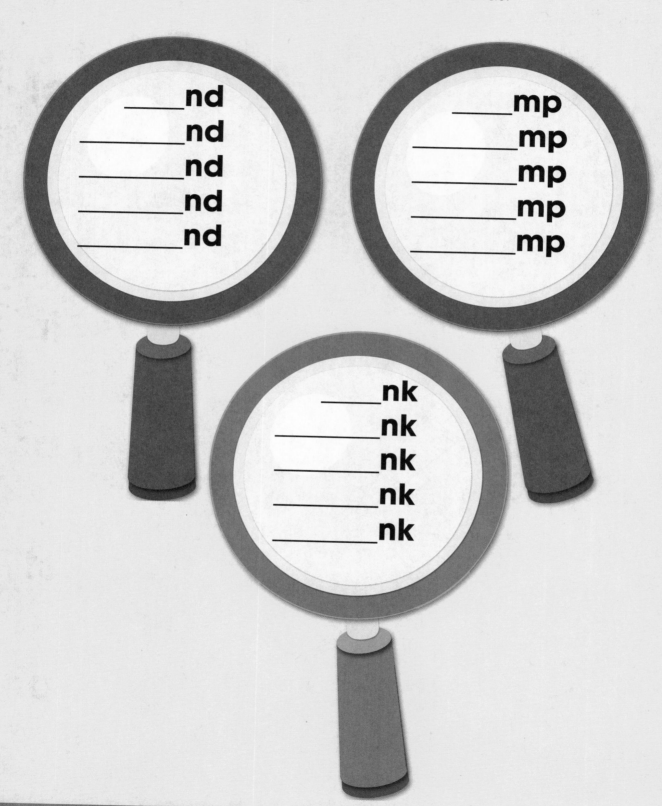

_____nd

_____nd

_____nd

_____nd

_____nd

_____mp

_____mp

_____mp

_____mp

_____mp

_____nk

_____nk

_____nk

_____nk

_____nk

Consonant Blends

Finish each sentence with a word from the word box. Then, draw a picture to show each sentence.

sting	prize	drank	plant	stamp

Tom _____ his water.

A bee can _____ you.

I put a _____ on my letter.

The _____ is green.

My story won first _____ .

Rhyming Words

Rhyming words are words that sound alike at the end of the word. **Cat** and **hat** rhyme.

Draw a circle around each word pair that rhymes. Draw an **X** on each pair that does not rhyme. Then, draw a picture of a word pair that rhymes.

soap
rope

red
dog

book
hook

cold
rock

cat
hat

yellow
black

one
two

rock
sock

rat
flat

Rhyming Words

Draw a line to match the pictures that rhyme. Write two of the rhyming word pairs below.

ABC Order

ABC order is the order in which letters come in the alphabet.

Put the words in ABC order. Write 1, 2, 3, 4, 5, or 6 in the box next to each animal's name. Then, color the pictures.

lion

monkey

giraffe

butterfly

frog

fish

Compound Words

Compound words are two words that are put together to make one new word.

Look at the pictures and the two words that are next to each other. Put the words together to make a new word. Write the new word.

_____

_____

_____

_____

_____

Names: Months of the Year

The months of the year begin with capital letters. Write the months of the year in order on pages 144 and 145. Be sure to use capital letters.

January

September

December

February

April

July

May

March

October

November

June

August

Names

Use a capital letter at the beginning of people's names.

Write your name.
Remember to use
a capital letter.

The days of the week begin with capital letters. Write the first letter
of each day of the week in the spaces below. Be sure to use capital
letters.

unday

onday

uesday

ednesday

hursday

riday

aturday

More Than One

An **s** at the end of a word often means there is more than one. Look at each picture. Circle the correct word. Write the word on the line.

two
bear   bears

four
pencil   pencils

one
sailboats   sailboat

three
tops   top

a
ball   balls

two
train   trains

Similarities: Objects

Color the picture in each row that is most like the first picture.

Classifying: Night and Day

Write the words from the box under the pictures they go with.

stars	light	dark	sun
night	rays	moon	day

Everything for Early Learning 1

Classifying: What Does Not Belong?

Draw an **X** on the word in each row that does not belong.

flashlight	candle	radio	fire
shirt	pants	coat	bat
cow	car	bus	train
beans	rice	ball	bread
gloves	hat	book	boots
fork	butter	cup	plate
book	ball	bat	water
dogs	bees	flies	ants

Classifying: Names, Numbers, Animals, Colors

Write the words from the box next to the words they describe. Then, draw and color a picture to show one of the words.

| Joe | Sue | dog | blue | pig | ten |
| two | cat | green | red | Tim | six |

Name Words
_____

Number Words
_____

Animal Words
_____

Color Words
_____

Sequencing: How Flowers Grow

Read the story. Then, write the steps to grow a flower.

Find a sunny spot. Then, plant a seed. Water it. The flower will start to grow. Pull the weeds around it. Remember to keep giving the flower water. Enjoy your flower.

Read about crayons. Then, write your answers.

Crayons come in many colors. Some crayons are dark colors. Some crayons are light colors. All crayons have wax in them.

How many colors of crayons are there?   many   few

Crayons come in _____ colors

and _____ colors.

What do all crayons have in them? _____

Read about snow. Circle the answers.

When you play in snow, dress warmly. Wear a coat. Wear a hat. Wear gloves. Do you wear these when you play in snow?

Snow is   warm.   cold.

When you play in snow, dress

warmly.   quickly.

List three things to wear when you play in snow.

_____

_____

_____

Read the passage. Then, finish the sentences.

Do you like cats? I do. To pet a cat, move slowly. Hold out your hand. The cat will come to you. Then, pet its head. Do not grab a cat! It will run away.

To pet a cat...

Move _____ .

Hold out your _____ .

The cat will come to _____ .

Pet the cat's _____ .

Do not _____ a cat!

Comprehension: Cats

Read the passage about cats again. Then, answer the questions.

What is a good title for the story?

The story tells you how to

What part of your body should you pet a cat with?

Why should you move slowly to pet a cat?

Why do you think a cat will run away if you grab it?

Classifying: Foods

Read the questions beside each plate. Draw three foods on each plate to answer the questions.

What foods can you cut with a knife?

What foods should you eat with a fork?

What foods can you eat with a spoon?

Comprehension: Rhymes

Read about words that rhyme. Then, circle the answers.

    Words that rhyme have the same ending sounds. *Wing* and *sing* rhyme. *Boy* and *toy* rhyme. *Dime* and *time* rhyme. Can you think of any other words that rhyme?

Words that rhyme have the same

    ending sounds.

    ending letters.

Time rhymes with

    tree.

    dime.

Write one rhyme for each word.

wing

boy

dime

pink

Read the passage. Then, answer the questions.

Let's Take a Trip!

Pack your bag. Shall we go by car, plane, or train? Let's go to the sea. When we get there, let's go on a sailboat.

What are three ways to travel?

Where will we go?

What will we do when we get there?

Making Inferences: Feelings

Read each passage. Choose a word from the box to show how each person feels.

| happy | excited | sad | mad |

Abby and Jen were best friends. Abby and her family moved far away. How does Abby feel?

_____

Deana could not sleep. It was the night before her birthday party. How does Deana feel?

_____

Jacob let his baby brother play with his teddy bear. His brother lost the bear. How does Jacob feel?

_____

Kia picked flowers for her mom. Her mom smiled when she got them. How does Kia feel?

_____

Books

What do you know about books? Use the words in the box below to help fill in the lines.

title illustrator fun	library author	glossary left to right

The name of the book is the _____.

_____ is the direction we read.

The person who wrote the words is the

_____.

Reading is _____!

There are many books in the _____.

The person who draws the pictures is the

_____.

The _____ is a kind of dictionary

in the book to help you find the meanings of words.

Nouns

A **noun** is a word that names a person, place, or thing. When you read a sentence, a noun is what the sentence is about.

Complete each sentence with a noun.

The _____ is tall.

My _____ is purple.

The _____ is jumping.

The _____ is cold.

Verbs are words that tell what a person or a thing can do.

The girl **pets** the dog.
The word **pets** is the verb. It shows action.

Draw a line between the verbs and the pictures that show action.
Then, color the pictures.

tie

grow

bake

build

brush

Nouns and Verbs

A **noun** is a person or thing a sentence tells about. A **verb** tells what the person or thing does.

Circle the noun in each sentence. Underline the verb.

Example: The (cat)sleeps.

The balloons float.

Children swim in the pool.

Apples grow on the tree.

The bird flies.

The cars drive.

Words That Describe

Describing words tell us more about a person, place, or thing.

Read the words in the box. Choose a word that describes each picture. Write the word next to the picture.

gray	round	tired	hot	tall

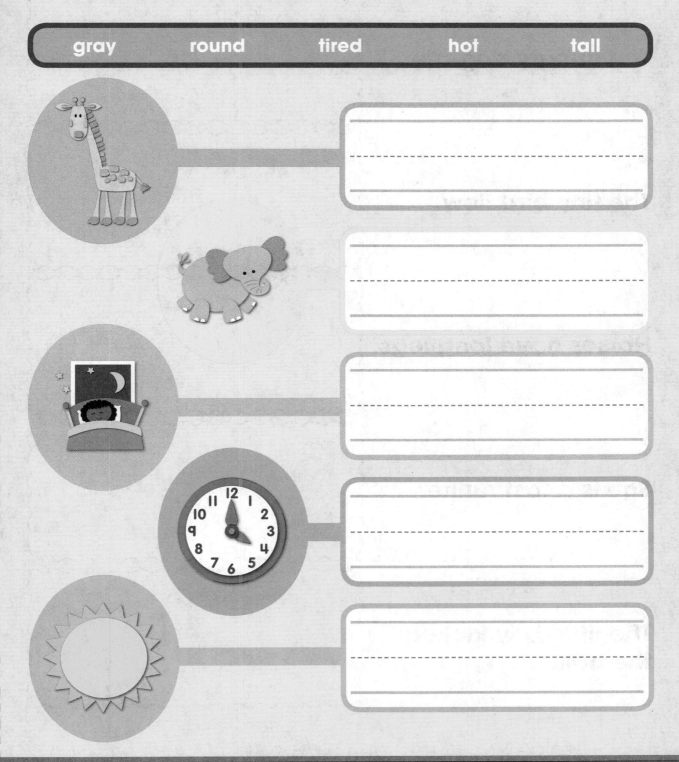

Everything for Early Learning 1

Words That Describe

Circle the describing word in each sentence. Draw a picture to show each sentence.

The hungry dog ate.

The tiny bird flew.

Horses have long legs.

She is a fast runner.

The little boy kicked the ball.

Words That Describe

Colors and numbers can describe nouns.

Underline the describing word in each sentence. Draw a picture to go with each sentence.

A yellow moon was in the sky.

Two worms are on the road.

The tree had red apples.

The girl wore a blue dress.

Sequencing: Comparative Adjectives

Look at each group of pictures. Write **1**, **2**, or **3** under each picture to show where it should be.

small _____   **smallest** _____   **smaller** _____

biggest _____   **big** _____   **bigger** _____

wider _____   **wide** _____   **widest** _____

Sequencing: Comparative Adjectives

Look at each group of pictures. Write **1**, **2**, or **3** under each picture to show where it should be.

shortest _____   **shorter** _____   **short** _____

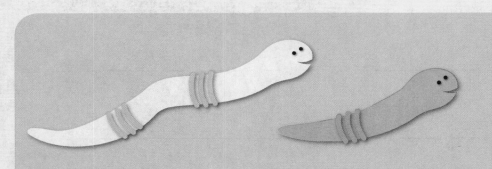

longest _____   **longer** _____   **long** _____

tall _____   **taller** _____   **tallest** _____

Everything for Early Learning   1

Synonyms

Find the synonyms that describe each picture. Write the words in the boxes below each picture.

small   run   large   bake   jog   little   big   cook

_____

_____

_____

_____

_____

_____

_____

_____

Similarities

Circle the word in each row that is most like the first word in the row.
Then, draw a picture to show each word.

grin	**smile**	**frown**	**mad**
bag	**jar**	**sack**	**box**
cat	**fruit**	**animal**	**flower**
apple	**rot**	**cookie**	**fruit**
around	**circle**	**square**	**dot**
brown	**tan**	**black**	**red**
bird	**dog**	**cat**	**duck**
bee	**fish**	**ant**	**snake**

Synonyms

Read each sentence and look at the underlined word. Circle the word that means the same thing. Write the circled words.

The <u>little</u> dog ran.   tall   funny   small

The <u>happy</u> girl smiled.   glad   sad   good

The bird is in the <u>big</u> tree.   green   pretty   tall

He was <u>nice</u> to me.   kind   mad   bad

The baby is <u>tired</u>.   sleepy   sad   little

Similarities: Synonyms

Read the story. Write a word on the line that means almost the same as the word under the line.

Dan went to the _____.
store

He wanted to buy _____.
food

He walked very _____.
quickly

The store had what he wanted.

He bought it using _____.
dimes

Instead of walking home, Dan _____.
jogged

Opposites

Opposites are things that are very different from each other.

Draw a line between the opposites. Then, draw a picture to show each word.

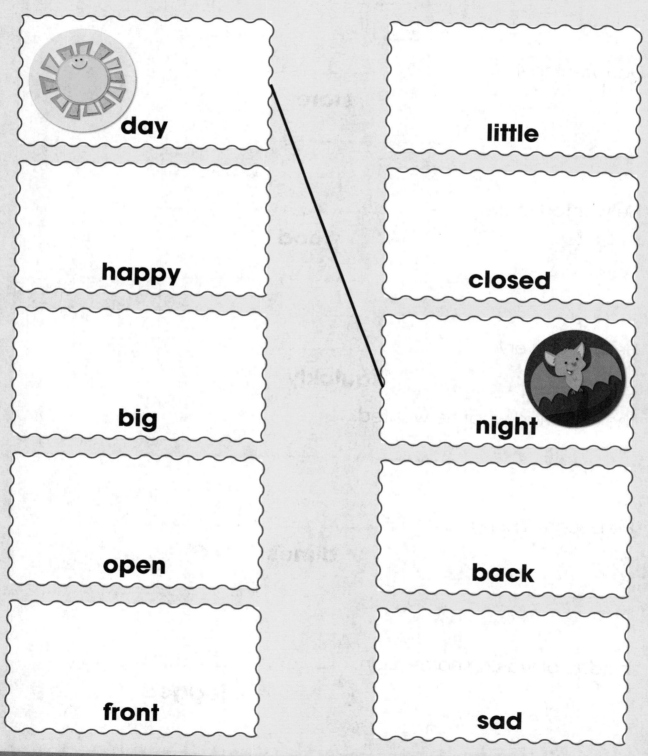

day

little

happy

closed

big

night

open

back

front

sad

Opposites

Draw lines to connect the words that are opposites.

up   wet

over   down

dry   dirty

clean   under

Opposites

Circle the two words in each sentence that are opposites.

Cold ice cream is good on a hot day.

Sam took off his wet socks and put on dry ones.

Do you like to swim fast or slow?

The dog is black and the cat is white.

The elephant looked really big next to the small mouse.

The tiny seed grew into a large plant.

Homophones

Homophones are words that **sound** the same but are spelled differently and mean something different. **Blew** and **blue** are homophones.

Read each sentence. Underline the two words that are homophones. Then, color the pictures.

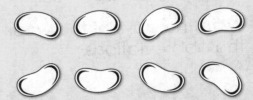

Tom ate eight jellybeans.

Sam read *Little Red Riding Hood*.

I kept one eye open.

The blue balloons blew in the wind.

We could see the sea from the beach.

Following Directions: Days of the Week

Calendars show the days of the week in order. Sunday comes first. Saturday comes last. There are five days in between. An **abbreviation** is a short way of writing words. The abbreviations for the days of the week are usually the first three or four letters of the word followed by a period.

Example: Sunday – Sun.

Write the days of the week in order on the calendar. Use the abbreviations.

Day 1
Sunday

Sun.

Day 2
Monday

Day 3
Tuesday

Tues.

Day 4
Wednesday

Day 5
Thursday

Thurs.

Day 6
Friday

Day 7
Saturday

Sentences

Sentences begin with capital letters.

Read the sentences and write them below. Begin each sentence with a capital letter.

Example:

the cat is fat.   The cat is fat.

the dinosaur is big.

the girl is sad.

bikes are fun!

dad can bake.

Word Order

Word order is the order of words in a sentence that makes sense.

Put the words in the correct order to make a sentence. Write the sentences on the lines below.

We made cake. some

good. It was

We the sold cake.

cost It 50 cents.

fun. We had

Word Order

Put the words in the correct order to make a sentence. Write the sentences on the lines below.

a Jan fish. has

Bill to swim. likes

The shining. sun is

sand. the in Jack plays

cold. water The is

Telling Sentences

Read the sentences and write them below. Begin each sentence with a capital letter. End each sentence with a period.

most children like pets

_____

some children like dogs

_____

some children like cats

_____

some children like fish

_____

some children like all animals

_____

Use the words in the box to write the first word of each asking sentence. Be sure to begin each question with a capital letter. End each question with a question mark.

_____ you like the zoo _____

_____ much does it cost _____

_____ you feed the ducks _____

_____ you see the monkeys _____

_____ time will you eat lunch _____

do
how
can
will
what

Asking Sentences

Read the asking sentences. Write the sentences below. Begin each sentence with a capital letter. End each sentence with a question mark.

what game will we play

do you like to read

how old are you

who is your best friend

can you tie your shoes

Put a period or a question mark at the end of each sentence below.

Do you like parades

The clowns lead the parade

Can you hear the band

The balloons are big

Can you see the horses

Is and Are

We use **is** in sentences about one person or one thing. We use **are** in sentences about more than one person or thing.

Example: The dog **is** barking.
The dogs **are** barking.

Write **is** or **are** in the sentences below. Then, draw a picture to show each sentence.

Jim _____ playing baseball.

Fred and Sam _____ good friends.

Cupcakes _____ my favorite treat.

Lisa _____ a good soccer player.

Is and Are

Write **is** or **are** in the sentences below. Then, draw a picture to show each sentence.

Cats and dogs _____ good pets.

Bill _____ my best friend.

Apples _____ good to eat.

We _____ going to the zoo.

Pedro _____ coming to my house.

When _____ you going to the zoo?

Read the words. Trace and write them on the lines. Then, circle the word that completes each sentence. Write the word on the line.

you and me

you and me

I will play with _____.   you   me

You can go with _____.   you   me

Can you run with _____?   you   me

Vocabulary

Read the words. Trace and write them on the lines. Then, circle the word that completes each sentence. Write the word on the line.

over over

under under

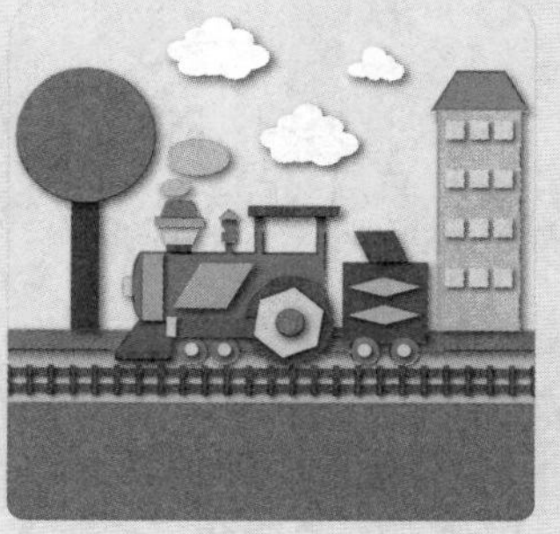

The clouds are ______________ the train.

over under

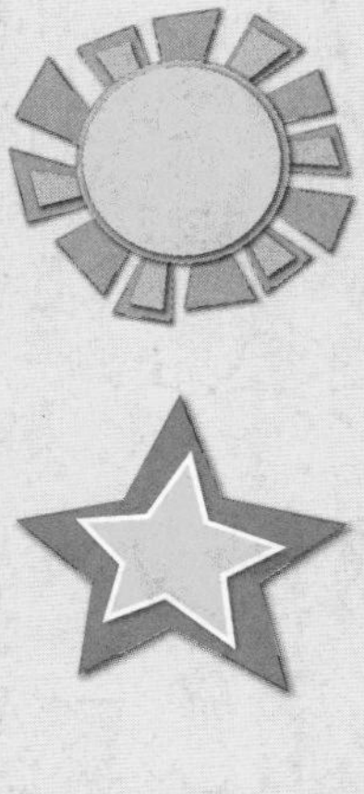

The star is ______________ the sun.

over under

Animal Names

Fill in the missing letters for each word. Then, color the pictures.

frog frog

fi___ f_sh

d_g _og

b__d _ir_

c_t _a_

A **sentence** tells about something.

These sentences tell about animals. Write the word that completes each sentence.

Example:

My ___frog___ jumps high.

I take my _____ for a walk.

My _____ lives in water.

My _____ can sing.

My _____ has a long tail.

Trace the letters to write the name of each thing. Write each name again by yourself. Then, color the pictures.

truck

car

van

plane

Things that Go: Sentences

These sentences tell about things that go. Write the word that completes each sentence.

The _____ is in the garage.

Dad's _____ had a flat tire.

The _____ flew high.

The _____ went fast.

Clothing Words

Trace the letters to write the name of each clothing word. Then, write each name again by yourself.

shirt   shirt

pants

vest

scarf

shoes

shorts

hat

Clothing Words: Sentences

Some of these sentences tell a whole idea. Others have something missing. If something is missing, draw a line to the word that completes the sentence. Put a period at the end of each sentence.

She is wearing a polka-dot   **holes**

The baseball player wore a

His pants were torn.

                                              dress

The socks had

The jacket had blue buttons.

The shoes were brown.   **hat**

Sentences

Write three sentences that tell about this picture. Begin each sentence with a capital letter and end it with a period.

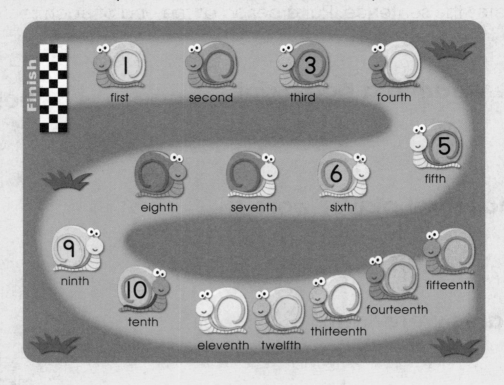

Food Names

Trace the letters to write the name of each food word. Write each name again by yourself. Then, color the pictures.

Example:

pear   pear

grapes

cheese

pizza

banana

Change each telling sentence into an asking sentence by changing the order of the words. Put a question mark at the end of each question.

Example:

The girl is eating.

Is the girl eating?

He is sharing.

He is drinking juice.

She is baking a cake.

Action Words

Circle the word that is spelled correctly. Then, write the correct spelling in the blank.

Example:

wass

(wash)

vash

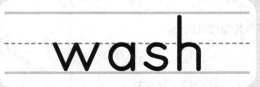
wash

seng

sinng

sing

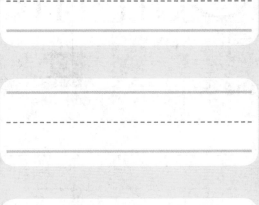

burn

birn

bern

smell

smel

smele

snile

smil

smile

silp

slip

slipp

Action Words: Asking Sentences

Write an asking sentence about each picture. Begin each sentence with **can**. Add an action word. Begin each asking sentence with a capital letter and end it with a question mark.

Example:

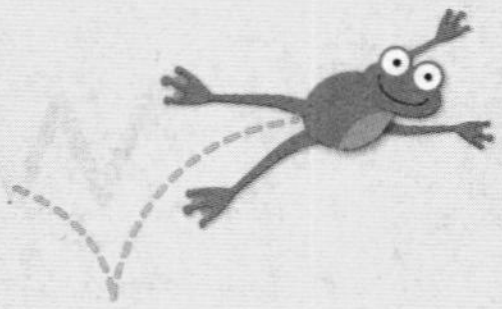

the frog can

Can the frog jump?

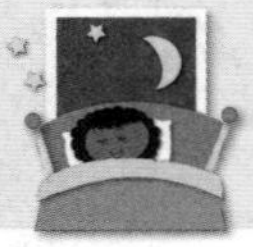

she can

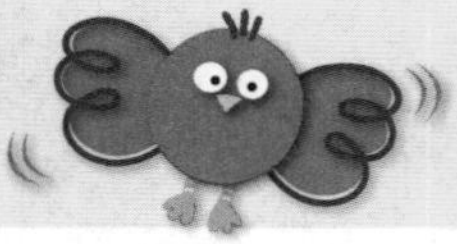

the bird can

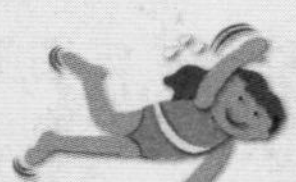

can she fast

Sentences

Write two telling sentences and one asking sentence about the picture. Put an action word in each sentence.

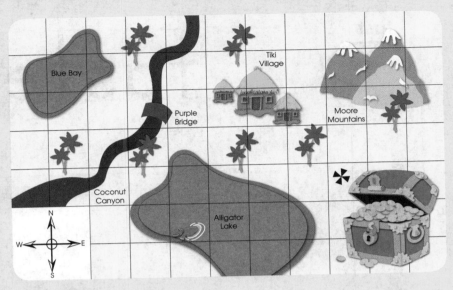

Two telling sentences:

One asking sentence:

Sense Words

Circle the word that is spelled correctly. Then, write the correct spelling in the blank.

Example:

tast

(taste)

tste

taste

touch

tuch

touh

smel

smll

smell

hre

hear

har

see

se

sae

Sense Words: More Than One

In each sentence, add **s** to show more than one. Then, write the sense word that completes each sentence.

Example:

The dog __s__ __taste__ the food.

see	touch	smell	hear

The flower _____ _____ good.

I can _____ five bee _____ .

The girl _____ _____ the frogs.

The boy _____ wanted to _____ the cactus.

Write an asking sentence about each picture. Begin each sentence with **can**. Add a sense word. Begin each asking sentence with a capital letter and end it with a question mark.

Example: can you the rain

Can you smell the rain?

can I the snail

can I the strawberry

can he the sun

can she the elephant

Sentences

Write two telling sentences and one asking sentence about this picture. Use a sense word in each sentence.

Two telling sentences:

One asking sentence:

Write the weather word that completes each sentence. Put a period at the end of the telling sentences and a question mark at the end of the asking sentences.

Example:

Do flowers grow in the ___ sun ___ ?

| rain | water | wet | hot |

The sun makes me ___ ___

When it rains, the grass gets ___ ___

Do you think it will ___ at our picnic ___

Should you drink the ___ from the rain ___

Weather Words: Completing a Story

Write the missing words to complete the story. The first letter of each word has been written for you.

"Please may I go outside?" I asked.

"It's too __c_____," my father told me.

"Maybe later the sun will come out." Later, the sun did come out.

Then, it began to __s_____ again. "May I go out now?" I asked again.

Dad looked out the window. "You will get __w_____," he said.

"But I want to see how much __s_____ there is to shovel," I said.

"You mean you want to __p_____ outside," Dad said with a smile.

How did Dad know that?

Sentences

Write two telling sentences about these pictures. Then, write an asking sentence about one of the pictures. Use the weather words and other words you know.

Telling sentences:

Asking sentence:

Fill in the missing letters for each word.

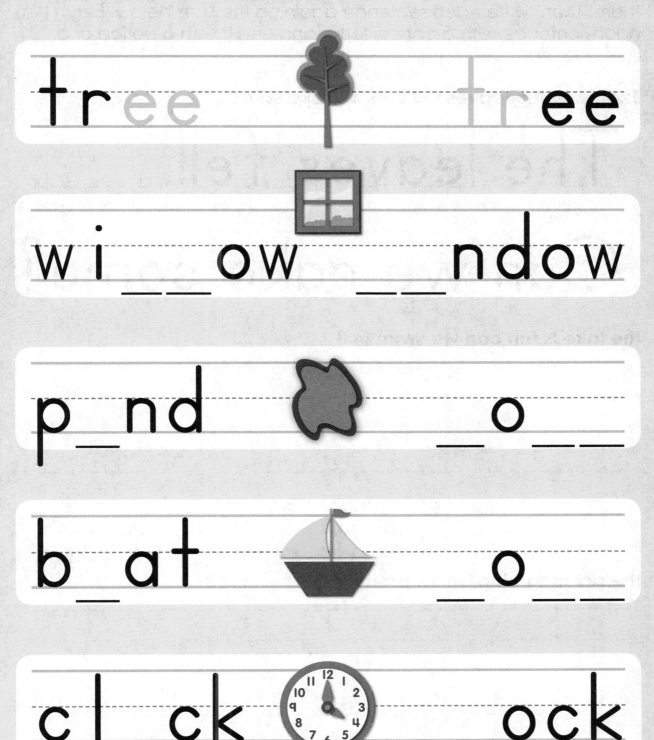

tr ee   tree

wi __ __ ow   __ __ ndow

p _ nd   __ __ __ o

b _ at   __ o __ __

cl _ ck   __ __ ock

My World: Sentences

Read the two sentences on each line and draw a line between them. Then, write each sentence again on the lines below. Begin each sentence with a capital letter and end it with a period or a question mark.

Example: the leaves fell|can we rake some

The leaves fell.

Can we rake some?

the lake is fun can we swim in it

the sky is so blue isn't it pretty

Sentences

Write two telling sentences about the picture. Then, write an asking sentence about the picture. Use words that tell about your world and other words you know.

Two telling sentences:

One asking sentence:

The Parts of My Body: Sentences

Read the sentence parts below. Draw a line from the first part of the sentence to the second part that completes it. Then, draw a picture to show each sentence.

I give big hugs   with my arms.

with my car.

My feet   drive the car.

got wet in the rain.

I have a bump   on my head.

on my coat.

My mittens   keep my arms warm.

keep my hands warm.

I can jump high   using my legs.

using a spoon.

Opposite Words

Some words are opposites. **Opposites** are things that are very different from each other. **Dark** and **light** are opposites.

Trace the letters to write each word. Write the word again by yourself. Then, draw a picture to show each set of words.

new   new

old

big

little

lost

found

Read the sentence. Then, write a sentence that tells the opposite.

Example: The dog is little.

The dog is big.

| found | new | first | lost | old | last |

Her book is lost.

The cat eats first.

I like my old hat.

Fill in the missing letters for each word. Then, draw a picture to show each word.

Example:

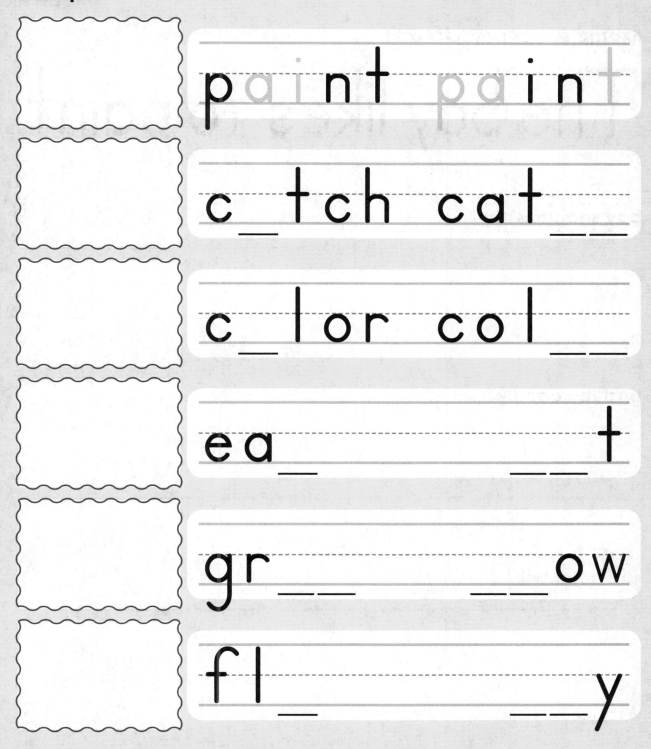

p a i n t   p a i n t

c _ t c h   c a t _ _

c _ l o r   c o l _ _

e a _ _ _ _ _ t _ _ _ t

g r _ _ _ _ _ _ _ o w

f l _ _ _ _ _ _ _ y

More Action Words: Sentences

Rewrite each sentence in the correct order. Remember to begin each sentence with a capital letter and end it with a period.

Example: likes boy to paint the

The boy likes to paint.

boy see grow the

bird the can fly

she color will

Use the action words you know to write sentences that tell about these pictures. Write a question about the last picture.

Example:

The trees grow.

Write a question about this picture.

People Words

Trace the letters to write each word. Then, write the word again by yourself.

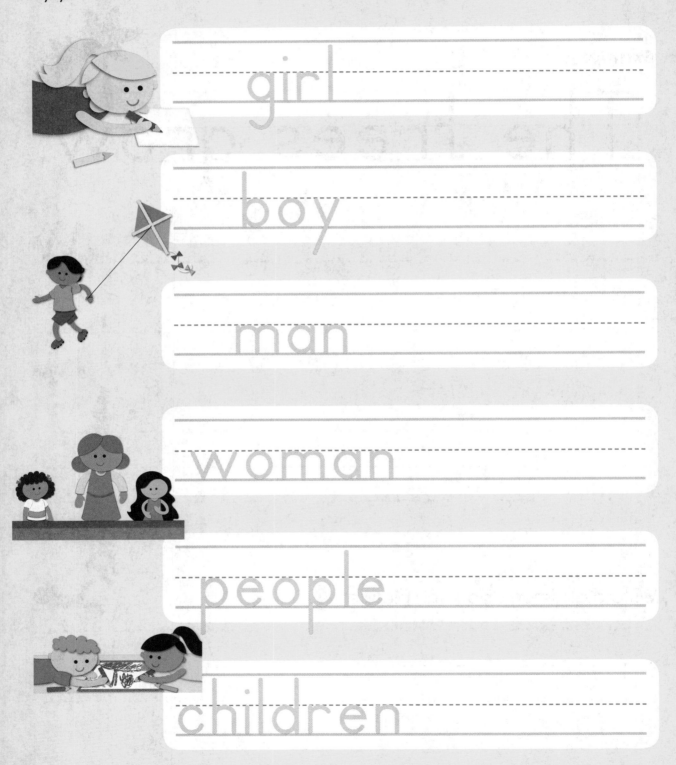

girl

boy

man

woman

people

children

People Words

Write a people word in each sentence to tell who is doing something.

The _____ played ball.

The _____ ran in the field.

The _____ had to do her homework.

The _____ washed the happy dog.

Some _____ like to bake.

People Words: Sentences

Write a people word that completes each sentence. Then, draw a picture to show each sentence.

| people | man | girl | children | boy | woman |

The _____ feeds the cat.

The _____ are buying dessert.

What is the _____ painting?

The _____ will grow corn.

The dog runs to the _____.

There are long lines of _____.

Answer Key

Cracker Count
Draw the correct number of crackers on each pan.

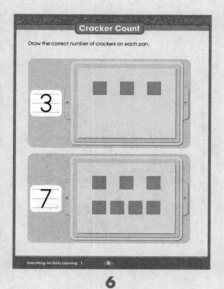

6

Catching Fish
Look at the number. Catch that number of fish by circling the fish in the pond.

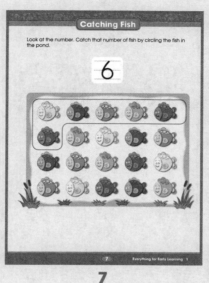

7

How Many Socks?
Count the socks in each row. Write the number of socks. Then, circle even or odd.

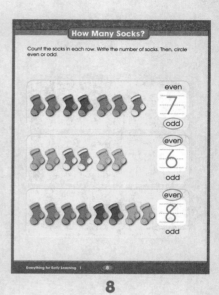

8

Balloon Bunches
Count the balloons. Write the number of tens and ones and the total. In the last box, draw balloons to show the tens and ones. Then, write the total.

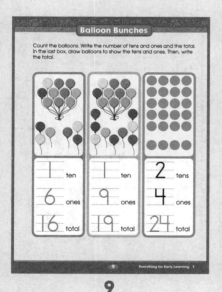

9

Balloon Bunches
Count the balloons. Write the number of tens and ones and the total. In the last box, draw balloons to show the tens and ones. Then, write the total.

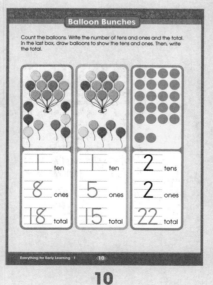

10

Pinball Numbers
Write numbers to complete the chart. The first one has been done for you.

11

Answer Key

Pinball Numbers
Write numbers to complete the charts.

Peas and Carrots
Count the peas and carrots. Circle groups of 10. Write how many tens and ones. Write the total. Then, answer the question.

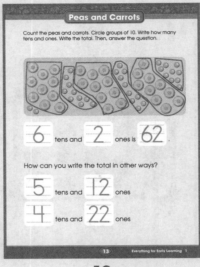

6 tens and 2 ones is 62.

How can you write the total in other ways?

5 tens and 12 ones

4 tens and 22 ones

Traffic Jam
Draw and color the correct cars. Write the missing number under each car.

- A red car is 1st.
- A blue car is 4th.
- A green car is 10th.
- A brown car is 3rd.
- A black car is 7th.
- A white car is 9th.

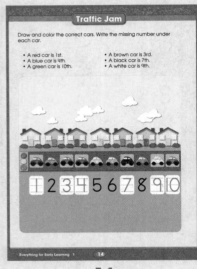

Speedy Snails
Write the number on each shell and the ordinal number word on each provided line to show the order the snails will finish the race.

Puppy Playtime
Help the puppy count to 100. Write the number that is hidden under each object.

Square Subtraction
Use the hundred board to solve each problem. Circle the first number in the problem on the board. Then, draw a path on the board as you count back to subtract the second number. Draw a triangle around the answer. Write the answer to complete the number sentence.

22 − 11 = 11   67 − 14 = 53   36 − 9 = 27

88 − 12 = 76   94 − 5 = 89   51 − 12 = 39

Answer Key

Filling Flower Beds

Look at the number. Draw flowers in the 2 flower beds to show the number.

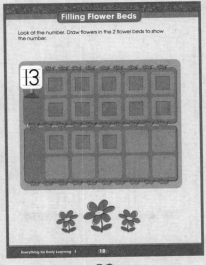

18

The More Door

Draw a door around the number that is greater on each house.

19

The More Door

Draw a door around the number that is greater on each house.

20

TV Sets

Read each number. Circle the correct number word. Show the number in 2 different ways using pictures, number sentences, or tally marks.

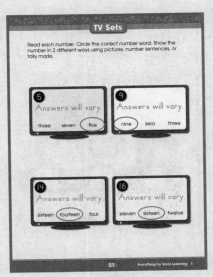

21

Bubble Counts

Count the bubbles in each bathtub. Write the number on the line. Circle the correct number word.

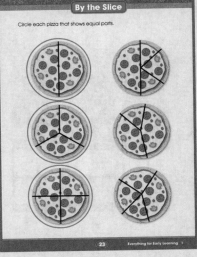

22

By the Slice

Circle each pizza that shows equal parts.

23

Answer Key

Fraction Snacks

Draw lines to divide each snack into equal parts to show the bottom number of the fraction. Draw an X on one part to show the fraction.

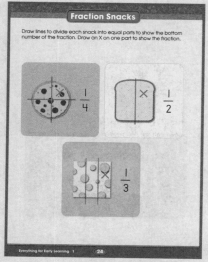

24

Fraction Snacks

Draw lines to divide each snack into equal parts to show the bottom number of the fraction. Draw an X on one part to show the fraction.

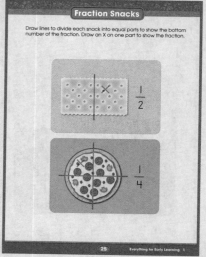

25

Apple Picking

Write the fractions of red and yellow apples in each tree. The first two have been started for you.

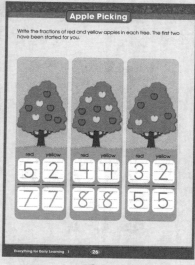

26

Apple Picking

Write the fractions of red and yellow apples in each tree.

27

Nest Sets

Look at the numbers on the first and second nests. Draw eggs in the nests to show the numbers. Draw the correct number of eggs in the last nest to make the sum. Write the sum.

$$4 + 3 = 7$$

28

Nest Sets

Write a number below the first and second nests. Draw eggs in the nests to show the numbers. Draw the correct number of eggs in the last nest to make the sum. Write the sum.

Answers will vary.

29

Answer Key

Planting On

Count the vegetables in each row. Draw the correct number of vegetables to make the sum at the end of each row.

12

9

14

30

Planting On

Count the vegetables in each row. Draw the correct number of vegetables to make the sum at the end of each row.

11

8

13

31

Bears' Lair

Draw 8 bears in the cave. Roll a die and subtract that many bears. Write the number sentence. Repeat three more times.

Answers will vary.

32

Bears' Lair

Draw 10 bears in the cave. Roll a die and subtract that many bears. Write the number sentence. Repeat three more times.

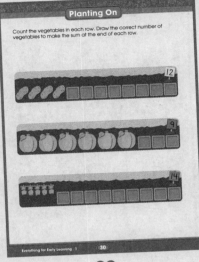

Answers will vary.

33

Frogs on a Log

Roll a die. Starting at 10, count back the rolled number as hops on the log. Write what you did as a subtraction fact. Repeat five more times.

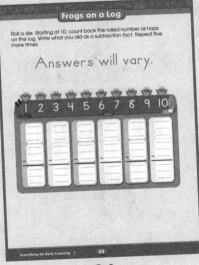

Answers will vary.

34

How Many More?

Count the gumballs in the pair of gumball machines. Write a number sentence to show how many more gumballs are in the first machine.

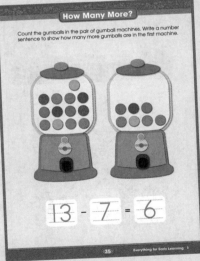

$13 - 7 = 6$

35

Answer Key

Blastoff Facts

Write the four facts for each fact family.

6, 9, 15

$6 + 9 = 15$
$9 + 6 = 15$
$15 - 9 = 6$
$15 - 6 = 9$

4, 8, 12

$4 + 8 = 12$
$8 + 4 = 12$
$12 - 8 = 4$
$12 - 4 = 8$

36

Seeing Spots

Look at the domino in each box. Each domino represents a fact family. Write the related facts for each fact family.

$5 + 4 = 9$
$4 + 5 = 9$
$9 - 5 = 4$
$9 - 4 = 5$

$6 + 2 = 8$
$2 + 6 = 8$
$8 - 6 = 2$
$8 - 2 = 6$

37

Basket of Cherries

Three children picked cherries. Add the three amounts of cherries that each child picked.

Jan

5
2
+ 5
12

Ruby

6
4
+ 1
11

Uri

7
2
+ 3
12

38

Mystery Signs

Write + or – to make each number sentence true.

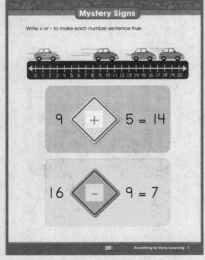

$9 \; + \; 5 = 14$

$16 \; - \; 9 = 7$

39

Mystery Signs

Write + or – to make each number sentence true.

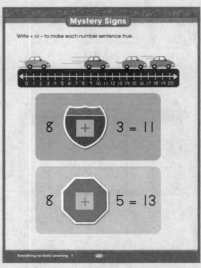

$8 \; + \; 3 = 11$

$8 \; + \; 5 = 13$

40

Let's Share

Count the acorns and peanuts. Divide each set of nuts into two equal groups so that the squirrels will have equal shares. Draw the nuts.

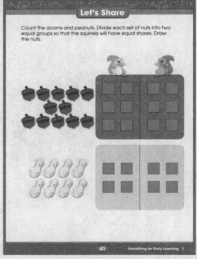

41

Answer Key

42

Count on to solve each problem. The common sum is the spot where the pirate buried his treasure. Mark the spot on the number line with an X.

10	14	16	11	9	15
+ 8	+ 4	+ 2	+ 7	+ 9	+ 3
18	18	18	18	18	18

Everything for Early Learning 1   42

42

43

Adventure Island

Count on to solve each problem. The common sum is the spot where the pirate buried his treasure. Mark the spot on the number line with an X.

10	12	14	11	8	13
+ 6	+ 4	+ 2	+ 5	+ 8	+ 3
16	16	16	16	16	16

43   Everything for Early Learning 1

43

44

Flip It!

Solve each addition problem. Use the addition facts to help you solve each subtraction problem.

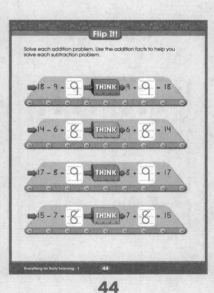

18 – 9 = **9**   THINK   9 + **9** = 18

14 – 6 = **8**   THINK   6 + **8** = 14

17 – 8 = **9**   THINK   8 + **9** = 17

15 – 7 = **8**   THINK   7 + **8** = 15

Everything for Early Learning 1   44

44

45

Flip It!

Solve each addition problem. Use the addition facts to help you solve each subtraction problem.

18 – 8 = **10**   THINK   8 + **10** = 18

14 – 5 = **9**   THINK   5 + **9** = 14

17 – 6 = **11**   THINK   6 + **11** = 17

15 – 4 = **11**   THINK   4 + **11** = 15

45   Everything for Early Learning 1

45

46

More or Less

Start with the middle number. Write the numbers that are 1 more and 2 more. Then, write the numbers that are 1 less and 2 less.

–2	–1		+1	+2
5	6	7	8	9
8	9	10	11	12
13	14	15	16	17

Everything for Early Learning 1   46

46

47

Two Color Sums

Use two different colors of crayons to color each row. Then, write two addition facts that show the color amounts.

Answers will vary.

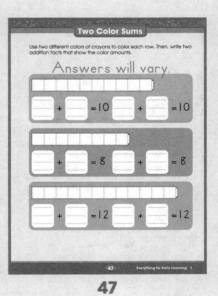

___ + ___ = 10   ___ + ___ = 10

___ + ___ = 8   ___ + ___ = 8

___ + ___ = 12   ___ + ___ = 12

47   Everything for Early Learning 1

47

Answer Key

Dip Into Dominoes

Count the dots on each side of each domino. Then, write the related facts for each domino.

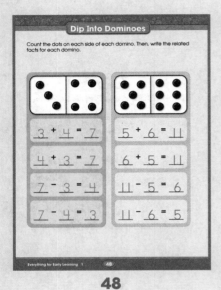

3 + 4 = 7   5 + 6 = 11

4 + 3 = 7   6 + 5 = 11

7 - 3 = 4   11 - 5 = 6

7 - 4 = 3   11 - 6 = 5

48

Subtraction Squares

Subtract each row and then each column. Write the answers on the lines.

11	6	5
3	2	1
8	4	4

14	7	7
5	4	1
9	3	6

16	8	8
9	4	5
7	4	3

49

Subtraction Squares

Subtract each row and then each column. Write the answers on the lines.

10	4	6
3	2	1
7	2	5

13	8	5
5	4	1
8	4	4

15	7	8
9	4	5
6	3	3

50

Jelly Bean Math

Draw or cross out jelly beans in each frame to make the number.

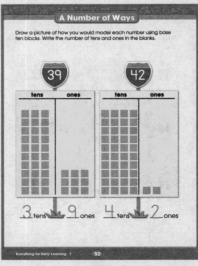

Make 9   Make 6

51

A Number of Ways

Draw a picture of how you would model each number using base ten blocks. Write the number of tens and ones in the blanks.

39   42

tens   ones   tens   ones

3 tens 9 ones   4 tens 2 ones

52

A Number of Ways

Draw a picture of how you would model each number using base ten blocks. Write the number of tens and ones in the blanks.

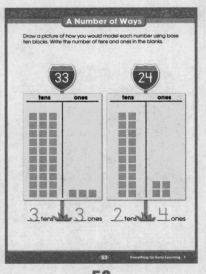

33   24

tens   ones   tens   ones

3 tens 3 ones   2 tens 4 ones

53

Answer Key

Zero the Hero

Write each missing number to complete the addition facts with zero.

$11 + 0 = 11$

$16 + 0 = 16$

$0 + 20 = 20$

54

Bubble, Bubble

Color each pair of bubbles that have the same sum. Use a different color for each pair.

55

Seesaw Sums

Draw stars on each side of the seesaw to test each equation. Circle the equations that are true. Cross out the equations that are not true.

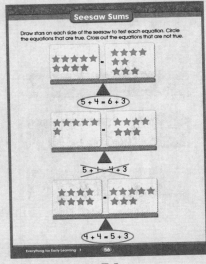

$5 + 4 = 6 + 3$

$5 + 1 = 4 + 3$

$4 + 4 = 5 + 3$

56

Tipping the Scales

Look at the numbers below each scale. Write >, <, or = to compare each set of numbers.

> greater than   **<** less than   **=** equal to

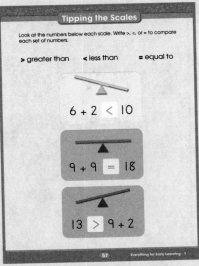

$6 + 2 < 10$

$9 + 9 = 18$

$13 > 9 + 2$

57

Something Fishy

Choose two characteristics. Write them on the lines. Sort the fish by writing their numbers in the bowls.

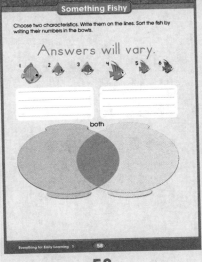

Answers will vary.

both

58

Odd Ones Out

Draw an X on the object in each row that does not belong.

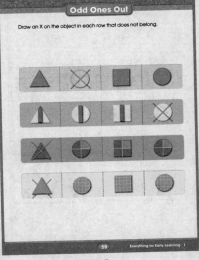

59

Answer Key

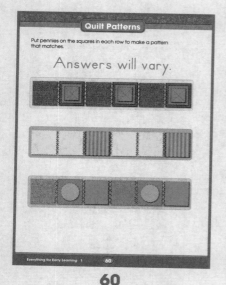

60

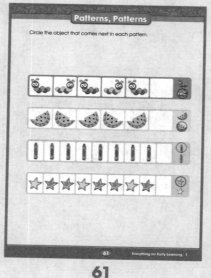

61

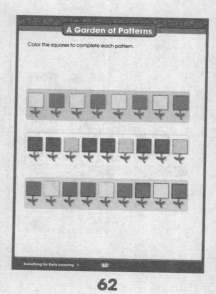

62

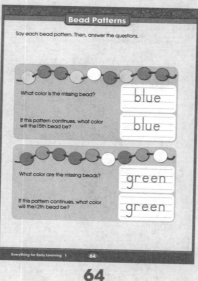

63

Bead Patterns

64

65

Answer Key

Patterns Rule!

Each child named the shape pattern in a different way. Explain each child's rule.

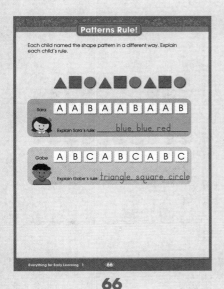

Sara: A A B A A B A A B

Explain Sara's rule: _blue, blue, red_

Gabe: A B C A B C A B C

Explain Gabe's rule: _triangle, square, circle_

Everything for Early Learning 1   66

66

Growing Patterns

Finish each pattern.

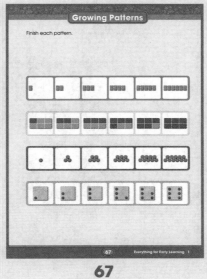

67   Everything for Early Learning 1

67

What's the Rule?

Draw what comes next in each pattern.

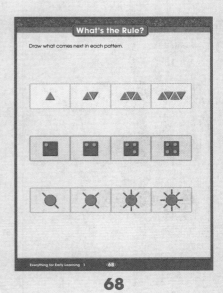

Everything for Early Learning 1   68

68

Puppy Patterns

Name each pattern using letters. Then, draw and color dogs to copy the pattern.

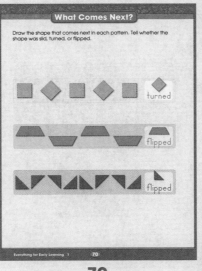

A A B A A B

A B C A B C

69   Everything for Early Learning 1

69

What Comes Next?

Draw the shape that comes next in each pattern. Tell whether the shape was slid, turned, or flipped.

turned

flipped

flipped

Everything for Early Learning 1   70

70

Bead a Pattern

Color the blank beads to continue each pattern.

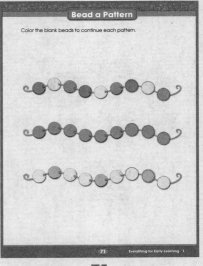

71   Everything for Early Learning 1

71

Answer Key

Going Up!

Finish each pattern.

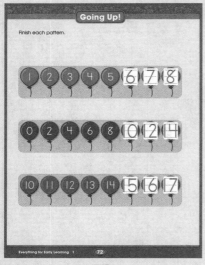

Petal Patterns

Study each number pattern. Start at the dot. Write the rule.

Buzzing Around

Write the missing numbers in each row of flowers.

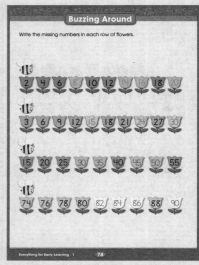

Name that Figure!

Circle the word that describes each object.

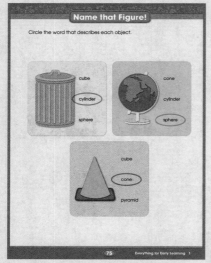

Name that Figure!

Circle the word that describes each object.

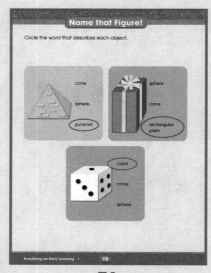

Shapes Rule!

Draw some shapes by each rule. Then, write your own sorting rules and sort the shapes.

Answer Key

The Great Shape Sort

Follow the directions.

1. Color each circle.
2. Outline each shape that has 4 sides.
3. Circle each small shape.
4. Draw an X on each square.
5. Draw a dot in each shape with 3 sides.

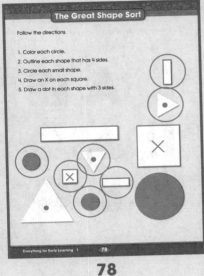

78

Angles, Faces, and Sides

Read each description. Circle the correct figure. You may circle more than one figure in each row.

six sides
two faces
no angles
six faces
three angles

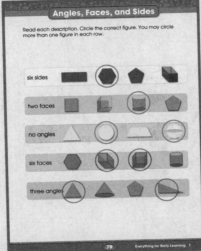

79

Stack and Roll

Look at each figure. Decide if it will roll, stack, or do both. Circle the answer(s).

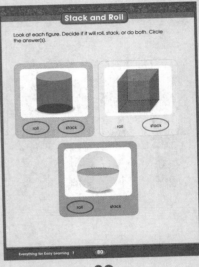

roll   stack
roll   stack
roll   stack

80

Shape Creations

Circle the shapes needed to make each picture.

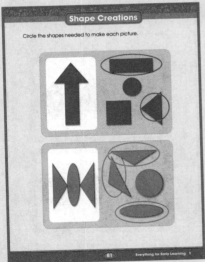

81

Castle Shapes

Describe where each shape is. Use color words, shape names, and position words.

Answers will vary.

82

Beth's Beagle

Follow the directions to help Beth find her dog. Write the missing words in the directions as you go. Draw an X where she finds the dog.

Walk past 2 trees. Turn right and walk to the house.

Turn left and walk to the **rocks**

Turn right and walk to the **pond**
Turn right and walk past the pond.

Turn right and walk to the **garden**
Turn left and walk to the end of the garden.
Turn left and walk straight to find the dog.

The dog is in the **doghouse**

83

Answer Key

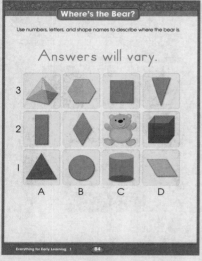

84

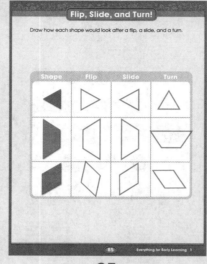

85

86

87

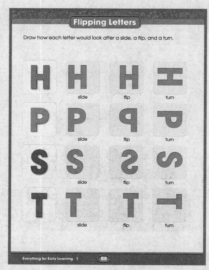

88

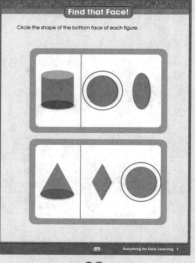

89

Answer Key

Picnic Perimeters

Write how many total steps it will take for each ant to walk around his picnic blanket.

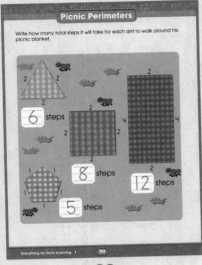

6 steps

8 steps

12 steps

5 steps

90

Will's Worms

Will found some worms in his backyard. Use two fingers at a time to measure each worm.

Answers will vary.

two-finger widths

two-finger widths

two-finger widths

two-finger widths

91

Know Your Units

Circle the unit of measurement that best measures each object.

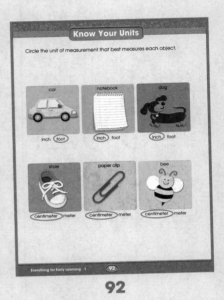

car — inch (foot)
notebook — (inch) foot
dog — (inch) foot

shoe — (centimeter) meter
paper clip — (centimeter) meter
bee — (centimeter) meter

92

Ribbon Measurement

Use the width of your thumb to measure the length of each ribbon.

Answers will vary.

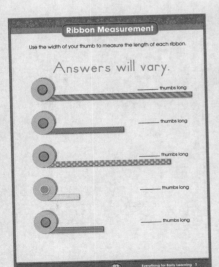

_____ thumbs long

_____ thumbs long

_____ thumbs long

_____ thumbs long

_____ thumbs long

93

Order Up!

Number the events from 1 to 6 in the order in which they occur.

Eat breakfast. **2**

Eat lunch. **4**

Go to bed. **6**

Go to school. **3**

Wake up. **1**

Eat dinner. **5**

94

The Hands of Time

Draw the hands or write the numbers to show the time for each clock.

12:00   7:00   3:30   10:30   6:00   9:00   4:30   8:30

95

Answer Key

The Hands of Time

Draw the hands or write the numbers to show the time for each clock.

2:00 · 4:00
5:00 · 8:00
2:30 · 3:30
11:30 · 7:30

96

Time and Time Again

Read the times. Draw the hands and write the numbers for each time given.

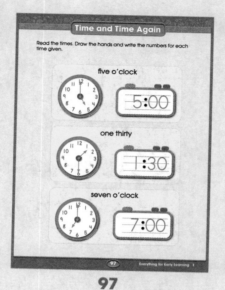

five o'clock — 5:00
one thirty — 1:30
seven o'clock — 7:00

97

Time and Time Again

Read the times. Draw the hands and write the numbers for each time given.

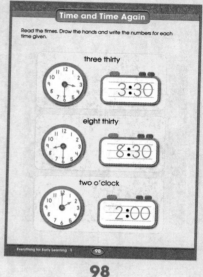

three thirty — 3:30
eight thirty — 8:30
two o'clock — 2:00

98

Elapsed Laps

Read each word problem. Draw the hands on the first clock to show the start time for the swimmer's laps. Draw the hands on the last clock to show the end time for the laps.

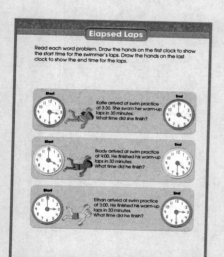

Katie arrived at swim practice at 3:30. She swam her warm-up laps in 30 minutes. What time did she finish?

Brady arrived at swim practice at 4:00. He finished his warm-up laps in 30 minutes. What time did he finish?

Ethan arrived at swim practice at 3:00. He finished his warm-up laps in 30 minutes. What time did he finish?

99

Elapsed Laps

Read each word problem. Draw the hands on the first clock to show the start time for the swimmer's laps. Draw the hands on the last clock to show the end time for the laps.

Jen arrived at swim practice at 4:30. She swam her warm-up laps in 30 minutes. What time did she finish?

Scott arrived at swim practice at 5:00. He finished his warm-up laps in 30 minutes. What time did he finish?

Adam arrived at swim practice at 2:30. He finished his warm-up laps in 30 minutes. What time did he finish?

100

Ants to Elephants

Number the animals from 1 to 6 to order them from lightest to heaviest.

chicken 3
frog 2
elephant 6
ant 1
dog 4
cow 5

101

Answer Key

A Balancing Act

Write the names of two objects or draw two objects on each scale to make the picture true.

Answers will vary.

102

Shape Sorts

Draw shapes in each box that have something in common with the shape pictured.

Answers will vary.

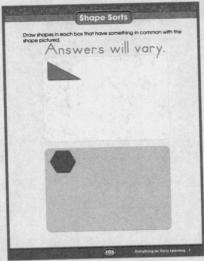

103

Pencil Poll Pictograph

Jon took a poll of four friends to see how many pencils each had in his or her pencil box. Use Jon's tally chart to draw the pencils in the graph.

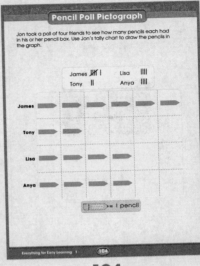

104

Backyard Bugs

Lin counted the bugs she collected in her backyard. Draw Xs in the spaces above each bug to make a bar graph of her data.

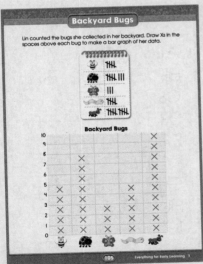

105

Picnic Time

Brian counted the items at the picnic. Draw Xs in the spaces above each item to make a bar graph of his data.

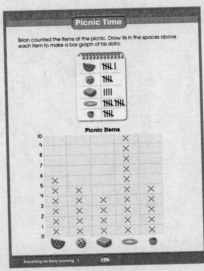

106

Preferred Pets

Look at the results of a class survey about favorite pets. Draw smiley faces to show the data in a pictograph. Look at the key to see how many votes each smiley face stands for.

107

Answer Key

Animal Graphs

Study the graph. Then, answer the questions.

Answers will vary.

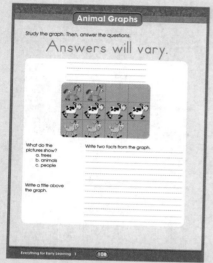

What do the pictures show?
a. trees
b. animals
c. people

Write two facts from the graph.

Write a title above the graph.

108

Sunny, Cloudy, or Rainy?

Mr. Kent's class kept track of the daily weather on the calendar last month. Use the calendar to answer the questions.

April

How many days were rainy? **10**

How many days were cloudy but not rainy? **6**

How many days were sunny? **14**

How many days are in the month? **30**

109

Likely or Unlikely?

Circle likely or unlikely to answer each question.

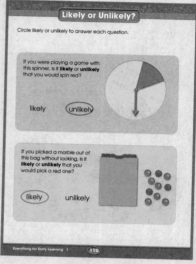

If you were playing a game with this spinner, is it **likely** or **unlikely** that you would spin red?

likely   (unlikely)

If you picked a marble out of this bag without looking, is it **likely** or **unlikely** that you would pick a red one?

(likely)   unlikely

110

Wishing Well

Decide how likely it is that a tossed coin will land on each well. Below each well, write more likely, likely, or less likely.

more likely   likely   less likely

111

Name, Address, Phone

This book belongs to

Answers will vary.

I live at

The city I live in is

The state I live in is

My phone number is

113

Review the Alphabet

Practice writing the letters.

Aa Aa Aa Aa Aa
Bb Bb Bb Bb Bb
Cc Cc Cc Cc Cc
Dd Dd Dd Dd Dd
Ee Ee Ee Ee Ee
Ff Ff Ff Ff Ff
Gg Gg Gg Gg Gg
Hh Hh Hh Hh Hh
Ii Ii Ii Ii Ii

114

Answer Key

Review the Alphabet
Practice writing the letters.

Review the Alphabet
Practice writing the letters.

Letter Recognition
In each set, match the lowercase letter to the uppercase letter.

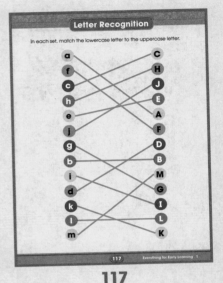

Letter Recognition
In each set, match the lowercase letter to the uppercase letter.

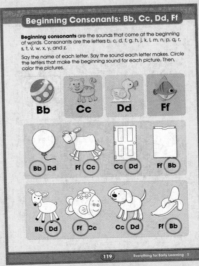

Beginning Consonants: Bb, Cc, Dd, Ff
Beginning consonants are the sounds that come at the beginning of words. Consonants are the letters b, c, d, f, g, h, j, k, l, m, n, p, q, r, s, t, v, w, x, y, and z.

Say the name of each letter. Say the sound each letter makes. Circle the letters that make the beginning sound for each picture. Then, color the pictures.

Beginning Consonants: Gg, Hh, Jj, Kk
Say the name of each letter. Say the sound each letter makes. Trace the letter pair that makes the beginning sound in each picture. Then, color the pictures.

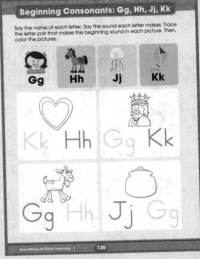

Answer Key

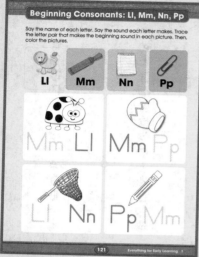

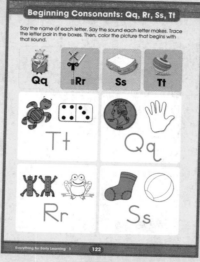

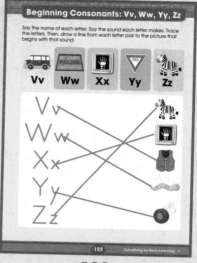

121

122

123

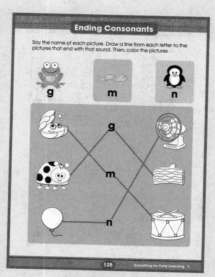

124

125

126

Answer Key

Ending Consonants: r, s, t, x

Say the name of each picture. Then, circle the ending sound for each picture.

Short Vowel Sounds

Vowels are the letters **a, e, i, o,** and **u.** Short **a** is the sound you hear in **ant.** Short **e** is the sound you hear in **elephant.** Short **i** is the sound you hear in **igloo.** Short **o** is the sound you hear in **octopus.** Short **u** is the sound you hear in **umbrella.**

Write **a, e, i, o,** or **u** in each blank to finish the word. Draw a line from the word to the picture. Then, color the pictures.

pot
map
tent
duck
kids

Long Vowel Sounds

Vowels are the letters **a, e, i, o,** and **u.** Long vowel sounds say their own names. Long **a** is the sound you hear in **hay.** Long **e** is the sound you hear in **me.** Long **i** is the sound you hear in **pie.** Long **o** is the sound you hear in **no.** Long **u** is the sound you hear in **cute.**

Write **a, e, i, o,** or **u** in each blank to finish the word. Draw a line from the word to the picture. Then, color the pictures.

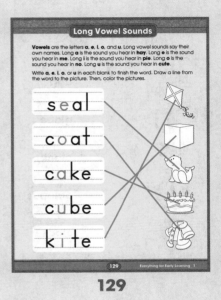

seal
coat
cake
cube
kite

127

128

129

Short and Long Aa

Short **a** sounds like the **a** in **hat.** Long **a** sounds like the **a** in **cape.**

Say the name of each picture. If it has the short **a** sound, color it **red.** If it has the long **a** sound, color it **yellow.**

Short and Long Ee

Short **e** sounds like the **e** in **hen.** Long **e** sounds like the **e** in **bee.**

Say the name of each picture. Circle the pictures that have the short **e** sound. Draw a triangle around the pictures that have a long **e** sound. Then, color the pictures.

Short and Long Ii

Short **i** sounds like the **i** in **pig.** Long **i** sounds like the **i** in **kite.**

Say the name of each picture. If it has the short **i** sound, color it **yellow.** If it has the long **i** sound, color it **red.**

130

131

132

Answer Key

133

Short and Long Oo

Short **o** sounds like the **o** in **dog**. Long **o** sounds like the **o** in **rope**. Draw a line from the picture to the word that names it. Draw a circle around the word if it has a short **o** sound.

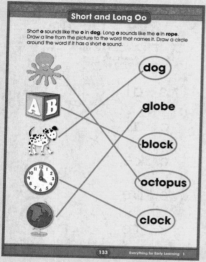

dog
globe
block
octopus
clock

133

134

Short and Long Uu

Short **u** sounds like the **u** in **bug**. Long **u** sounds like the **u** in **blue**.

Say the name of each picture. If it has the short **u** sound, color it **green**. If it has the long **u** sound, color it **purple**.

134

135

Vowels

Write the correct vowel on the line to complete each word.

a e i o u

c a t   d o g

g i f t   b i b

s u n   c o w

s n o w   g o a t

135

136

Consonant Blends

Consonant blends are two or more consonant sounds together in a word. The blend is made by combining the consonant sounds.

Example: floor

The name of each picture begins with a **blend**. Circle the beginning blend for each picture. Then, color the pictures.

bl fl (cl)   cl (fl) gl   fl (bl) pl

fl cl (gl)   (pl) gl cl   gl fl (cl)

136

137

Consonant Blends

Draw a line from the picture to the blend that begins its name. Then, color the pictures.

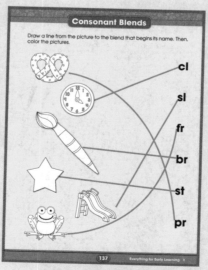

cl
sl
fr
br
st
pr

137

138

Ending Consonant Blends

Add letters to the word endings to create new words.

_nd   _mp
ba_nd   bu_mp
ha_nd   du_mp
la_nd   ju_mp
sa_nd   pu_mp

_nk
ba_nk
ra_nk
sa_nk
ta_nk

Possible answers:

138

Answer Key

Consonant Blends

Finish each sentence with a word from the word box. Then, draw a picture to show each sentence.

| sting | prize | drank | plant | stamp |

Tom **drank** his water.

A bee can **sting** you.

I put a **stamp** on my letter.

The **plant** is green.

My story won first **prize**.

Drawings will vary.

139

Rhyming Words

Rhyming words are words that sound alike at the end of the word. **Cat** and **hat** rhyme.

Draw a circle around each word pair that rhymes. Draw an **X** on each pair that does not rhyme. Then, draw a picture of a word pair that rhymes.

soap rope — red dog (X) — book hook

cold rock (X) — cat hat — yellow black (X)

one two (X) — rock sock — rat flat

Drawings will vary.

140

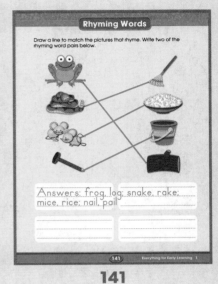

Rhyming Words

Draw a line to match the pictures that rhyme. Write two of the rhyming word pairs below.

Answers: frog, log; snake, rake; mice, rice; nail, pail

141

ABC Order

ABC order is the order in which letters come in the alphabet.

Put the words in ABC order. Write 1, 2, 3, 4, 5, or 6 in the box next to each animal's name. Then, color the pictures.

lion **5**   monkey **6**   giraffe **4**

butterfly **1**   frog **3**   fish **2**

142

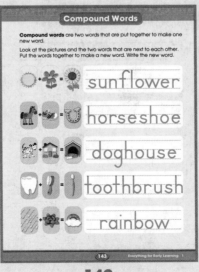

Compound Words

Compound words are two words that are put together to make one new word.

Look at the pictures and the two words that are next to each other. Put the words together to make a new word. Write the new word.

sunflower

horseshoe

doghouse

toothbrush

rainbow

143

Names: Months of the Year

The months of the year begin with capital letters. Write the months of the year in order on pages 144 and 145. Be sure to use capital letters.

January
September
December
February
April
July
May
March
October
November
June
August

January
February
March
April
May
June

144

Answer Key

Names: Months of the Year

- July
- August
- September
- October
- November
- December

145

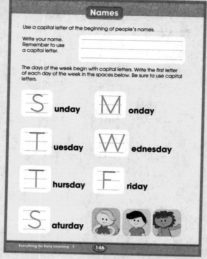

Names

Use a capital letter at the beginning of people's names.

Write your name. Remember to use a capital letter.

The days of the week begin with capital letters. Write the first letter of each day of the week in the spaces below. Be sure to use capital letters.

- **S** unday
- **M** onday
- **T** uesday
- **W** ednesday
- **T** hursday
- **F** riday
- **S** aturday

146

More Than One

An **s** at the end of a word often means there is more than one. Look at each picture. Circle the correct word. Write the word on the line.

- two — bear (bears) → bears
- four — pencil (pencils) → pencils
- one — sailboats (sailboat) → sailboat
- three — (tops) top → tops
- a — (ball) balls → ball
- two — train (trains) → trains

147

Similarities: Objects

Color the picture in each row that is most like the first picture.

148

Classifying: Night and Day

Write the words from the box under the pictures they go with.

| stars | light | dark | sun |
| night | rays | moon | day |

- stars
- moon
- dark
- night
- sun
- rays
- light
- day

149

Classifying: What Does Not Belong?

Draw an **X** on the word in each row that does not belong.

flashlight	candle	~~radio~~	fire
shirt	pants	coat	~~box~~
~~car~~	car	bus	train
beans	rice	~~ball~~	bread
gloves	hat	~~book~~	boots
fork	~~butter~~	cup	plate
book	ball	bat	~~water~~
~~dogs~~	bees	flies	ants

150

Answer Key

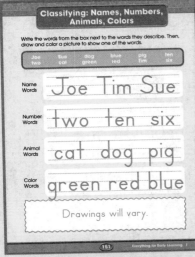

Classifying: Names, Numbers, Animals, Colors

Write the words from the box next to the words they describe. Then, draw and color a picture to show one of the words.

| Joe | Sue | dog | blue | pig | ten |
| two | cat | green | red | Tim | six |

Name Words: Joe Tim Sue

Number Words: two ten six

Animal Words: cat dog pig

Color Words: green red blue

Drawings will vary.

151

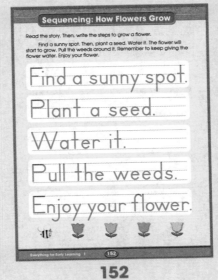

Sequencing: How Flowers Grow

Read the story. Then, write the steps to grow a flower.

Find a sunny spot. Then, plant a seed. Water it. The flower will start to grow. Pull the weeds around it. Remember to keep giving the flower water. Enjoy your flower.

Find a sunny spot.

Plant a seed.

Water it.

Pull the weeds.

Enjoy your flower.

152

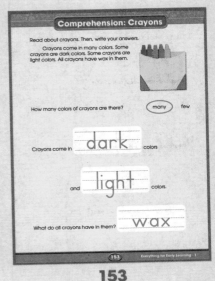

Comprehension: Crayons

Read about crayons. Then, write your answers.

Crayons come in many colors. Some crayons are dark colors. Some crayons are light colors. All crayons have wax in them.

How many colors of crayons are there? (many) few

Crayons come in dark colors

and light colors.

What do all crayons have in them? wax

153

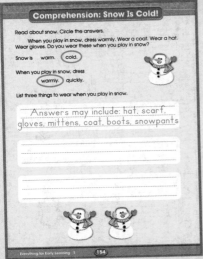

Comprehension: Snow Is Cold!

Read about snow. Circle the answers.

When you play in snow, dress warmly. Wear a coat. Wear a hat. Wear gloves. Do you wear these when you play in snow?

Snow is warm. (cold.)

When you play in snow, dress (warmly.) quickly.

List three things to wear when you play in snow.

Answers may include: hat, scarf, gloves, mittens, coat, boots, snowpants

154

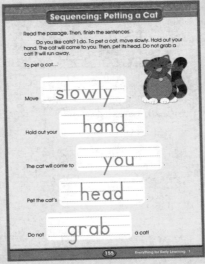

Sequencing: Petting a Cat

Read the passage. Then, finish the sentences.

Do you like cats? I do. To pet a cat, move slowly. Hold out your hand. The cat will come to you. Then, pet its head. Do not grab a cat! It will run away.

To pet a cat...

Move slowly

Hold out your hand

The cat will come to you

Pet the cat's head

Do not grab a cat!

155

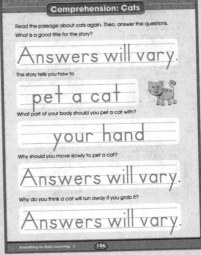

Comprehension: Cats

Read the passage about cats again. Then, answer the questions.

What is a good title for the story?

Answers will vary.

The story tells you how to

pet a cat

What part of your body should you pet a cat with?

your hand

Why should you move slowly to pet a cat?

Answers will vary.

Why do you think a cat will run away if you grab it?

Answers will vary.

156

Answer Key

Classifying: Foods

Read the questions beside each plate. Draw three foods on each plate to answer the questions.

Answers will vary.

What foods can you cut with a knife?

What foods should you eat with a fork?

What foods can you eat with a spoon?

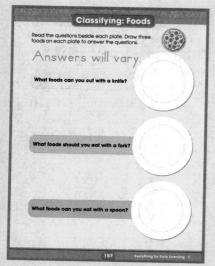

Comprehension: Rhymes

Read about words that rhyme. Then, circle the answers.

Words that rhyme have the same ending sounds. *Wing* and *sing* rhyme. *Boy* and *toy* rhyme. *Dime* and *time* rhyme. Can you think of any other words that rhyme?

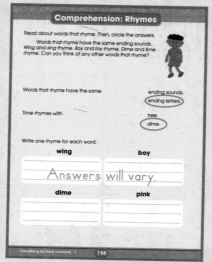

Words that rhyme have the same ~~ending sounds.~~
(ending letters.)

Time rhymes with ~~tree.~~
(dime.)

Write one rhyme for each word.

wing	boy
Answers	will vary.
dime	**pink**

158

Comprehension: Travel

Read the passage. Then, answer the questions.

Let's Take a Trip!

Pack your bag. Shall we go by car, plane, or train? Let's go to the sea. When we get there, let's go on a sailboat.

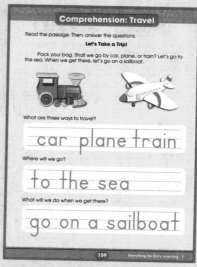

What are three ways to travel?

car plane train

Where will we go?

to the sea

What will we do when we get there?

go on a sailboat

159

Making Inferences: Feelings

Read each passage. Choose a word from the box to show how each person feels.

| happy | excited | sad | mad |

Abby and Jen were best friends. Abby and her family moved far away. How does Abby feel?

sad

Deana could not sleep. It was the night before her birthday party. How does Deana feel?

excited

Jacob let his baby brother play with his teddy bear. His brother lost the bear. How does Jacob feel?

mad

Kia picked flowers for her mom. Her mom smiled when she got them. How does Kia feel?

happy

160

Books

What do you know about books? Use the words in the box below to help fill in the lines.

title	library	glossary
illustrator	author	left to right
fun		

The name of the book is the title

Left to right is the direction we read.

The person who wrote the words is the author

Reading is fun

There are many books in the library

The person who draws the pictures is the illustrator

The glossary is a kind of dictionary in the book to help you find the meanings of words.

161

Nouns

A **noun** is a word that names a person, place, or thing. When you read a sentence, a noun is what the sentence is about.

Complete each sentence with a noun.

The giraffe is tall.

My flower is purple.

The frog is jumping.

The penguin is cold.

162

Answer Key

Verbs

Verbs are words that tell what a person or a thing can do.

The girl **pets** the dog.
The word **pets** is the verb. It shows action.

Draw a line between the verbs and the pictures that show action. Then, color the pictures.

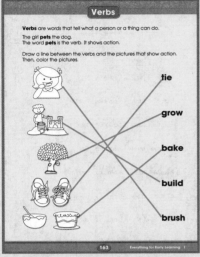

tie

grow

bake

build

brush

163

Nouns and Verbs

A **noun** is a person or thing a sentence tells about. A **verb** tells what the person or thing does.

Circle the noun in each sentence. Underline the verb.

Example: The (cat) sleeps.

The (balloons) float.

(Children) swim in the pool.

(Apples) grow on the tree.

The (bird) flies.

The (cars) drive.

164

Words That Describe

Describing words tell us more about a person, place, or thing.

Read the words in the box. Choose a word that describes each picture. Write the word next to the picture.

gray	round	tired	hot	tall

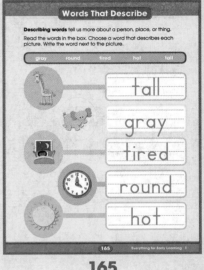

tall

gray

tired

round

hot

165

Words That Describe

Circle the describing word in each sentence. Draw a picture to show each sentence.

The (hungry) dog ate.

The (tiny) bird flew.

Horses have (long) legs.

She is a (fast) runner.

The (little) boy kicked the ball.

Drawings will vary.

166

Words That Describe

Colors and numbers can describe nouns.

Underline the describing word in each sentence. Draw a picture to go with each sentence.

A <u>yellow</u> moon was in the sky.

<u>Two</u> worms are on the road.

The tree had <u>red</u> apples.

The girl wore a <u>blue</u> dress.

Drawings will vary.

167

Sequencing: Comparative Adjectives

Look at each group of pictures. Write **1**, **2**, or **3** under each picture to show where it should be.

small _1_   smallest _3_   smaller _2_

biggest _3_   big _1_   bigger _2_

wider _2_   wide _1_   widest _3_

168

Answer Key

Sequencing: Comparative Adjectives

Look at each group of pictures. Write 1, 2, or 3 under each picture to show where it should be.

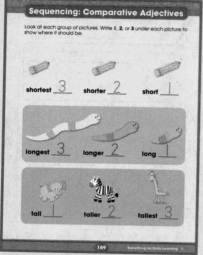

shortest **3**   shorter **2**   short **1**

longest **3**   longer **2**   long **1**

tall **1**   taller **2**   tallest **3**

169

Synonyms

Find the synonyms that describe each picture. Write the words in the boxes below each picture.

small   run   large   bake   jog   little   big   cook

small
little

large
big

run
jog

bake
cook

170

Similarities

Circle the word in each row that is most like the first word in the row. Then, draw a picture to show each word.

grin	(smile)	frown	mad
bag	jar	(sack)	box
cat	fruit	(animal)	flower
apple	rot	cookie	(fruit)
around	(circle)	square	dot
brown	(tan)	black	red
bird	dog	cat	(duck)
bee	fish	(ant)	snake

Drawings will vary.

171

Synonyms

Read each sentence and look at the underlined word. Circle the word that means the same thing. Write the circled words.

The **little** dog ran.   tall   funny   (small)

The **happy** girl smiled.   (glad)   sad   good

The bird is in the **big** tree.   green   pretty   (tall)

He was **nice** to me.   (kind)   mad   bad

The baby is **tired**.   (sleepy)   sad   little

small   glad   tall

kind   sleepy

172

Similarities: Synonyms

Read the story. Write a word on the line that means almost the same as the word under the line.

Dan went to the ___
store

He wanted to buy ___
food

He walked very ___
quickly

The store had what he wanted.

Answers will vary.

He bought it using ___
dimes

Instead of walking home, Dan ___
jogged

173

Opposites

Opposites are things that are very different from each other. Draw a line between the opposites. Then, draw a picture to show each word.

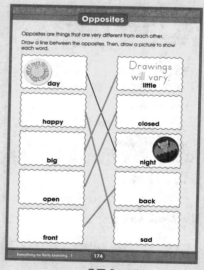

day

Drawings will vary.
little

happy

closed

big

night

open

back

front

sad

174

Answer Key

Opposites

Draw lines to connect the words that are opposites.

up — down
over — under
dry — wet
clean — dirty

175

Opposites

Circle the two words in each sentence that are opposites.

(Cold) ice cream is good on a (hot) day.

Sam took off his (wet) socks and put on (dry) ones.

Do you like to swim (fast) or (slow)?

The dog is (black) and the cat is (white).

The elephant looked really (big) next to the (small) mouse.

The (tiny) seed grew into a (large) plant.

176

Homophones

Homophones are words that **sound** the same but are spelled differently and mean something different. **Blew** and **blue** are homophones.

Read each sentence. Underline the two words that are homophones. Then, color the pictures.

Tom <u>ate</u> <u>eight</u> jellybeans.

Sam <u>read</u> Little <u>Red</u> Riding Hood.

I kept <u>one</u> <u>eye</u> open.

The <u>blue</u> balloons <u>blew</u> in the wind.

We could <u>see</u> the <u>sea</u> from the beach.

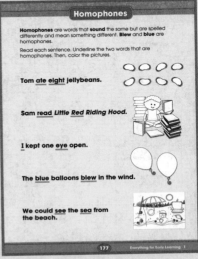

177

Following Directions: Days of the Week

Calendars show the days of the week in order. Sunday comes first. Saturday comes last. There are five days in between. An **abbreviation** is a short way of writing words. The abbreviations for the days of the week are usually the first three or four letters of the word followed by a period.

Example: Sunday – Sun.

Write the days of the week in order on the calendar. Use the abbreviations.

Day 1 Sunday	Day 2 Monday	Day 3 Tuesday
Sun.	Mon.	Tues.
Day 4 Wednesday	Day 5 Thursday	Day 6 Friday
Wed.	Thurs.	Fri.
	Day 7 Saturday	
	Sat.	

178

Sentences

Sentences begin with capital letters.

Read the sentences and write them below. Begin each sentence with a capital letter.

Example:
the cat is fat.   The cat is fat.

the dinosaur is big.

The dinosaur is big.

the girl is sad.

The girl is sad.

bikes are fun!

Bikes are fun!

dad can bake.

Dad can bake.

179

Word Order

Word order is the order of words in a sentence that makes sense.

Put the words in the correct order to make a sentence. Write the sentences on the lines below.

We made cake. some

We made some cake.

good. It was

It was good.

We the sold cake.

We sold the cake.

cost It 50 cents.

It cost 50 cents.

fun. We had

We had fun.

180

Answer Key

Word Order

Put the words in the correct order to make a sentence. Write the sentences on the lines below.

a Jan fish. has

Jan has a fish.

Bill to swim. likes

Bill likes to swim.

The shining. sun is

The sun is shining.

sand. the in Jack plays

Jack plays in the sand.

cold. water The is

The water is cold.

181

Telling Sentences

Read the sentences and write them below. Begin each sentence with a capital letter. End each sentence with a period.

most children like pets

Most children like pets.

some children like dogs

Some children like dogs.

some children like cats

Some children like cats.

some children like fish

Some children like fish.

some children like all animals

Some children like all animals.

182

Asking Sentences

Use the words in the box to write the first word of each asking sentence. Be sure to begin each question with a capital letter. End each question with a question mark.

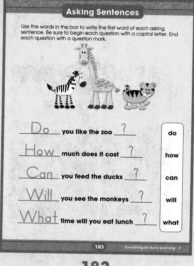

Do you like the zoo ?

How much does it cost ?

Can you feed the ducks ?

Will you see the monkeys ?

What time will you eat lunch ?

| do |
| how |
| can |
| will |
| what |

183

Asking Sentences

Read the asking sentences. Write the sentences below. Begin each sentence with a capital letter. End each sentence with a question mark.

what game will we play

What game will we play?

do you like to read

Do you like to read?

how old are you

How old are you?

who is your best friend

Who is your best friend?

can you tie your shoes

Can you tie your shoes?

184

Periods and Question Marks

Put a period or a question mark at the end of each sentence below.

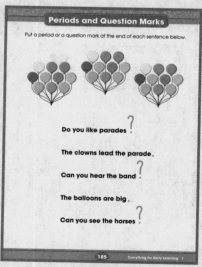

Do you like parades ?

The clowns lead the parade .

Can you hear the band ?

The balloons are big .

Can you see the horses ?

185

Is and Are

We use **is** in sentences about one person or one thing. We use **are** in sentences about more than one person or thing.

Example: The dog **is** barking.
The dogs **are** barking.

Write **is** or **are** in the sentences below. Then, draw a picture to show each sentence.

Jim __is__ playing baseball.

Fred and Sam __are__ good friends.

Cupcakes __are__ my favorite treat.

Lisa __is__ a good soccer player.

Drawings will vary.

186

Answer Key

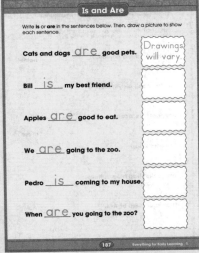

Is and Are

Write **is** or **are** in the sentences below. Then, draw a picture to show each sentence.

Cats and dogs __are__ good pets.

Bill __is__ my best friend.

Apples __are__ good to eat.

We __are__ going to the zoo.

Pedro __is__ coming to my house.

When __are__ you going to the zoo?

Drawings will vary.

187

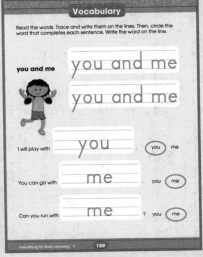

Vocabulary

Read the words. Trace and write them on the lines. Then, circle the word that completes each sentence. Write the word on the line.

you and me

you and me
you and me

I will play with __you__   (you) me

You can go with __me__ . you (me)

Can you run with __me__ ? you (me)

188

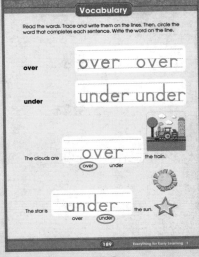

Vocabulary

Read the words. Trace and write them on the lines. Then, circle the word that completes each sentence. Write the word on the line.

over

over over

under

under under

The clouds are __over__ the train. (over) under

The star is __under__ the sun. over (under)

189

Animal Names

Fill in the missing letters for each word. Then, color the pictures.

frog frog

fish fish

dog dog

bird bird

cat cat

190

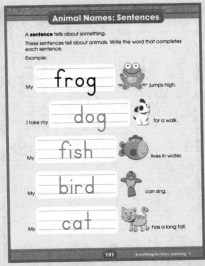

Animal Names: Sentences

A **sentence** tells about something.

These sentences tell about animals. Write the word that completes each sentence.

Example:

My __frog__ jumps high.

I take my __dog__ for a walk.

My __fish__ lives in water.

My __bird__ can sing.

My __cat__ has a long tail.

191

Things that Go

Trace the letters to write the name of each thing. Write each name again by yourself. Then, color the pictures.

truck truck

car   car

van   van

plane plane

192

Answer Key

Things that Go: Sentences

These sentences tell about things that go. Write the word that completes each sentence.

The **car** is in the garage.

Dad's **truck** had a flat tire.

The **plane** flew high.

The **van** went fast.

193

Clothing Words

Trace the letters to write the name of each clothing word. Then, write each name again by yourself.

shirt shirt
pants pants
vest vest
scarf scarf
shoes shoes
shorts shorts
hat hat

194

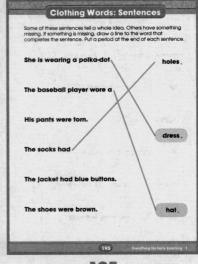

Clothing Words: Sentences

Some of these sentences tell a whole idea. Others have something missing. If something is missing, draw a line to the word that completes the sentence. Put a period at the end of each sentence.

She is wearing a polka-dot ——— holes .

The baseball player wore a ——— dress .

His pants were torn.

The socks had ———

The jacket had blue buttons.

The shoes were brown. ——— hat .

195

Sentences

Write three sentences that tell about this picture. Begin each sentence with a capital letter and end it with a period.

Answers will vary.

196

Food Names

Trace the letters to write the name of each food word. Write each name again by yourself. Then, color the pictures.

Example:

pear pear
grapesgrapes
cheesecheese
pizza pizza
bananabanana

197

Food Names: Asking Sentences

Change each telling sentence into an asking sentence by changing the order of the words. Put a question mark at the end of each question.

Example:

The girl is eating.

Is the girl eating?

He is sharing.

Is he sharing?

He is drinking juice.

Is he drinking juice?

She is baking a cake.

Is she baking a cake?

198

Answer Key

199

Action Words

Circle the word that is spelled correctly. Then, write the correct spelling in the blank.

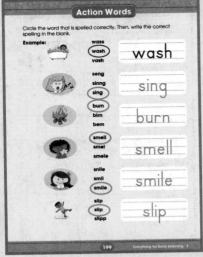

Example:

wass
(wash)
vash
→ wash

seng
sinng
(sing)
→ sing

(burn)
birn
bern
→ burn

(smell)
smel
smele
→ smell

smile
smil
(smile)
→ smile

(slip)
slip
slipp
→ slip

199 Everything for Early Learning 1

200

Action Words: Asking Sentences

Write an asking sentence about each picture. Begin each sentence with **can**. Add an action word. Begin each asking sentence with a capital letter and end it with a question mark.

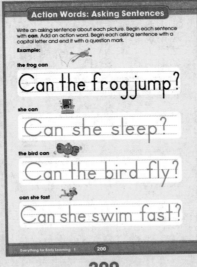

Example:

the frog can

Can the frog jump?

she can

Can she sleep?

the bird can

Can the bird fly?

can she fast

Can she swim fast?

Everything for Early Learning 1 200

201

Sentences

Write two telling sentences and one asking sentence about the picture. Put an action word in each sentence.

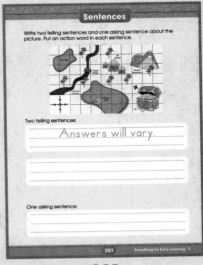

Two telling sentences:

Answers will vary.

One asking sentence:

201 Everything for Early Learning 1

202

Sense Words

Circle the word that is spelled correctly. Then, write the correct spelling in the blank.

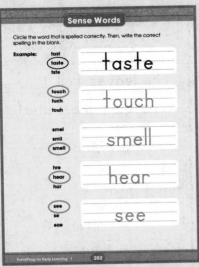

Example:

tast
(taste)
tste
→ taste

(touch)
tuch
touh
→ touch

smel
smil
(smell)
→ smell

hre
(hear)
har
→ hear

(see)
se
sae
→ see

Everything for Early Learning 1 202

203

Sense Words: More Than One

In each sentence, add **s** to show more than one. Then, write the sense word that completes each sentence.

Example:

The dog **s** taste the food.

see   touch   smell   hear

The flower **s** smell good.

I can see five bee **s**

The girl **s** hear the frogs.

The boy **s** wanted to touch the cactus.

203 Everything for Early Learning 1

204

Sense Words: Asking Sentences

Write an asking sentence about each picture. Begin each sentence with **can**. Add a sense word. Begin each asking sentence with a capital letter and end it with a question mark.

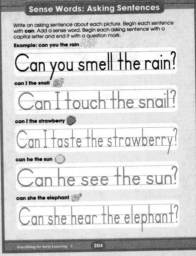

Example: can you the rain

Can you smell the rain?

can I the snail

Can I touch the snail?

can I the strawberry

Can I taste the strawberry?

can he the sun

Can he see the sun?

can she the elephant

Can she hear the elephant?

Everything for Early Learning 1 204

Answer Key

Sentences

Write three telling sentences and one asking sentence about this picture. Use a sense word in each sentence.

Three telling sentences:

Answers will vary.

One asking sentence:

205

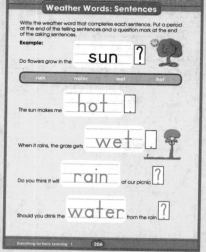

Weather Words: Sentences

Write the weather word that completes each sentence. Put a period at the end of the telling sentences and a question mark at the end of the asking sentences.

Example:

Do flowers grow in the   sun   ?

rain   water   wet   hot

The sun makes me   hot   .

When it rains, the grass gets   wet   .

Do you think it will   rain   at our picnic ?

Should you drink the   water   from the rain ?

206

Weather Words: Completing a Story

Write the missing words to complete the story. The first letter of each word has been written for you.

"Please may I go outside?" I asked.

"It's too   c old   ," my father told me.

"Maybe later the sun will come out." Later, the sun did come out.

Then, it began to   s now   again. "May I go out now?" I asked again.

Dad looked out the window. "You will get   w et   ." he said.

"But I want to see how much   s now   there is to shovel," I said.

"You mean you want to   p lay   outside." Dad said with a smile.

How did Dad know that?

207

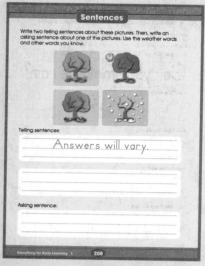

Sentences

Write two telling sentences about these pictures. Then, write an asking sentence about one of the pictures. Use the weather words and other words you know.

Telling sentences:

Answers will vary.

Asking sentence:

208

My World

Fill in the missing letters for each word.

tree   tree

wi nd ow   window

p on d   p on d

b oa t   b oa t

c l ock   c l ock

209

My World: Sentences

Read the two sentences on each line and draw a line between them. Then, write each sentence again on the lines below. Begin each sentence with a capital letter and end it with a period or a question mark.

Example: the leaves fell|can we rake some

The leaves fell.

Can we rake some?

the lake is fun|we swim in it

The lake is fun.

We swim in it.

the sky is so blue|isn't it pretty

The sky is so blue.

Isn't it pretty?

210

Answer Key

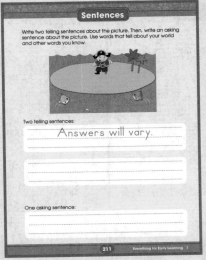

Sentences

Write two telling sentences about the picture. Then, write an asking sentence about the picture. Use words that tell about your world and other words you know.

Two telling sentences:

Answers will vary.

One asking sentence:

211

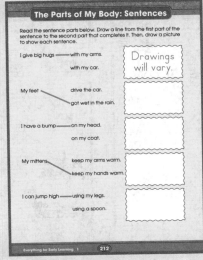

The Parts of My Body: Sentences

Read the sentence parts below. Draw a line from the first part of the sentence to the second part that completes it. Then, draw a picture to show each sentence.

I give big hugs —— with my arms.
with my car.

My feet —— drive the car.
got wet in the rain.

I have a bump —— on my head.
on my coat.

My mittens —— keep my arms warm.
keep my hands warm.

I can jump high —— using my legs.
using a spoon.

Drawings will vary.

212

Opposite Words

Some words are opposites. **Opposites** are things that are very different from each other. **Dark** and **light** are opposites.

Trace the letters to write each word. Write the word again by yourself. Then, draw a picture to show each set of words.

Drawings will vary.

new   new
old   old
big   big
little   little
lost   lost
found   found

213

Opposite Words: Sentences

Read the sentence. Then, write a sentence that tells the opposite.

Example: The dog is little.

The dog is big.

found   new   first   lost   old   last

Her book is lost.

Her book is found.

The cat eats first.

The cat eats last.

I like my old hat.

I like my new hat.

214

Action Words

Fill in the missing letters for each word. Then, draw a picture to show each word.
Example:

Drawings will vary.

paint   paint
catch   catch
color   color
eat   eat
grow   grow
fly   fly

215

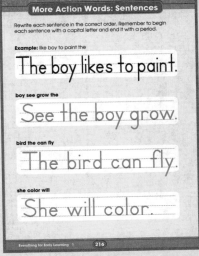

More Action Words: Sentences

Rewrite each sentence in the correct order. Remember to begin each sentence with a capital letter and end it with a period.

Example: like boy to paint the

The boy likes to paint.

boy see grow the

See the boy grow.

bird the can fly

The bird can fly.

she color will

She will color.

216

Answer Key

217

Sentences

Use the action words you know to write sentences that tell about these pictures. Write a question about the last picture.

Example:

The trees grow.

Answers will vary.

Write a question about this picture.

217   Everything for Early Learning 1

218

People Words

Trace the letters to write each word. Then, write the word again by yourself.

girl   girl

boy   boy

man   man

woman woman

people people

children children

Everything for Early Learning 1   218

219

People Words

Write a people word in each sentence to tell who is doing something.

The   boy   played ball.

The   children   ran in the field.

The   girl   had to do her homework.

The   woman   washed the happy dog.

Some   people   like to bake.

219   Everything for Early Learning 1

220

People Words: Sentences

Write a people word that completes each sentence. Then, draw a picture to show each sentence.

| people | man | girl | children | boy | woman |

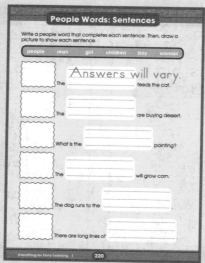

Answers will vary.

The _____ feeds the cat.

The _____ are buying dessert.

What is the _____ painting?

The _____ will grow corn.

The dog runs to the _____

There are long lines of _____

Everything for Early Learning 1   220